Janie,
are honored to
are Bill's memory
with you.
All my best,
Janis
Teegins
2003

HE GOT IT!

FUNDING MADE POSSIBLE BY

CLAYTON I. BENNETT
GRIFFIN COMMUNICATIONS, KWTV NEWS 9 & KOTV-6
OKLAHOMA CITY COMMUNITY FOUNDATION
OKLAHOMA STATE UNIVERSITY
EDDIE SUTTON

Kurt Atkinson
Ron Austin
Mr. and Mrs. Terry Bassett
Mr. and Mrs. Paul Bell
David Birchall
John Brooks
Suzanne Burks
Mr. and Mrs. J. D. Butts
Randy Cassimus
Mr. and Mrs. Dennis Clowers
Mr. and Mrs. David Cole
Bucky Conger
Carolyn Davis Conger
Mr. and Mrs. Kim Eccles and Family
Mr. and Mrs. Gary England
Hefner Middle School Students
Rodney E. Horton
Dan Ingham
Van Shea Iven
Steve Johnson
Mr. and Mrs. Jon N. King

Mr. and Mrs. Billy Lloyd
Mr. and Mrs. Ruben Millerborg
Mr. and Mrs. Aubie Price
Ruby Proctor
Mr. and Mrs. Hugo Schwartz
Kim Serrurier
Mr. and Mrs. Dean Sladek
Darryl Smette
Stacey D. Spivey
Mr. and Mrs. Tom Stockland
Mr. and Mrs. Max Thompson
Mr. and Mrs. Ed Tietgens
Jeff Tietgens
Mr. and Mrs. Scott Tietgens
Mr. and Mrs. William E. Tietgens
Mr. and Mrs. Jerry Vold
Stella Vold
Mr. and Mrs. Rick Wallenmeyer
Mr. and Mrs. Perry Wilson
Mr. and Mrs. Bob Winters
Mr. and Mrs. Scott Wray

FOREWORD BY EDDIE SUTTON

HE GOT IT!

My Life with Bill Teegins

Series Editor:
GINI MOORE CAMPBELL

Associate Editor:
ERIC DABNEY

Oklahoma Heritage Association
Oklahoma City

by **JANIS TEEGINS** with **BOB BURKE**

Printed in the United States of America.
ISBN 1-885596-35-9
Library of Congress Catalog Number 2003111385
Designed by Sandi Welch/2W Design Group
Unless otherwise noted, photographs are courtesy of the Bill Teegins family

OKLAHOMA HERITAGE ASSOCIATION
201 NORTHWEST FOURTEENTH STREET
OKLAHOMA CITY, OKLAHOMA 73103

table of contents

acknowledgments

*M*any people loved Bill Tietgens and graciously helped in gathering information and photographs for this book. Losing Bill was the most difficult challenge our family ever faced. He held God, his family, and others as most important in his life.

Bill would be embarrassed by all this attention, but he deserves memory and honor. Giving back was the best gift Bill had, and I hope this story inspires you to do the same.

Thanks to David Griffin and our KWTV family, including Kelly Ogle, Gary England, Ed Murray, Jenifer Reynolds, Terry Alexander, Jackie Mitchell, and Margie Kerley; Les Miles; Eddie Sutton; Kelvin Sampson; Bob Stoops; Ann Benjamin; Jon and Diane King; Sandy Marlin; Bob Losure; Clayton Vaughn; Joe Riddle; Rod Horton; my brother, Jim Gibson, and his wife, Charlene; Bill's parents, Bill and Carol Tietgens; my cousin, Sherry Sue Murray; John Rohde; Bob Hersom; Chris Harrison; Steve Buzzard; and the many other friends and colleagues of Bill who were more than happy to share stories and photographs.

I also thank my writing group, Oklahoma Write Now, for their listening hearts and helpful minds—with special thanks to Chalise Miner, who leads this merry band of writers and whose hand is on each page. I am grateful to Bev Binkowski, Joan Gilmore, M.J. Van Deventer, Ann Cameron, and Cathy Keating for leading me to Bob Burke.

Most of all, I thank the people of Oklahoma for their love and support during our time of grief and loss, and to my precious Amanda for her patience and help with the project.

I am indebted to our proofreaders—Judge Steven Taylor, George and Marcia Davis, David Hodges, Mike Jennings, George Baxter, Dave Tamez, John Hudson, Amanda Welch, and Stephanie Heck—and to Linda Lynn, Melissa Hayer, Mary Phillips, Robin Davison, and Billie Harry at the Oklahoma Publishing Company for help in selecting photographs.

Thanks to Eric Dabney and Stephanie Graves Ayala for editorial assistance, to Shelley Dabney and Amy Clakley for transcribing interviews, to Sandi Welch for a superb design of the book; to David Fitzgerald and Associates for the photography for the dust jacket, and to the Oklahoma Heritage Association and its chairman, Clay Bennett, and managing editor, Gini Moore Campbell, for their commitment to preserve Oklahoma's bold and exciting heritage.

This book is dedicated to our daughter, Amanda—the apple of her daddy's eye.

—JANIS TIETGENS

ncommon humility, unquestioned integrity, undaunted loyalty, and unparalleled ability are the best descriptives I could apply to my good friend Bill Teegins. It is a deep personal honor for me to write these few paragraphs as a foreword to a book about the life of someone who touched so many in a positive way.

Across our great state, all you have to do is mention Bill's name and you will find tens of thousands who call him their friend, even though they have only met him through their television screen. The impact Bill had on those who watched him or those who knew him personally was almost identical.

His humility was uncommon. Despite working in a profession where the landscape is dotted with larger-than-life egos, Bill displayed unbelievable humility. It appeared to be almost embarrassing when people would approach him for an autograph or a picture or just the opportunity to be able to go home and say they had met Bill Teegins.

Bill met few strangers. He was easy to engage in conversation, especially about baseball, the sport he most loved to talk about. He was equally at ease in the company of sports legends or the average fan. And, whether legend or fan, they were at ease with him.

His integrity was unquestioned. Bill was truly a professional journalist—he didn't report fiction. When he went with a story, you could be assured it was extensively researched and factual. He took his job seriously and when he had to report bad news, he did so with a sensitivity rarely found in his profession.

His integrity earned respect from every corner. There are two sports journalists from Oklahoma in recent memory who could sit in the office of a head coach at OSU in the morning and in the office of a head coach at OU in the afternoon and be respected in both places. One is the late Bill Conners, former sports editor of the *Tulsa World*. The other is Bill.

His loyalty was undaunted. In the all too brief time Bill spent as radio voice of Cowboy basketball, there was never a doubt that his loyalty was with the Orange and Black. He worked hard to develop relationships with players, coaches, and fans. Even though we knew he had to wear two hats—one as our radio voice and the other as sports director at KWTV—Bill was and always will be a member of the Oklahoma State athletic family.

He was up when we won and down when we lost. Even after a disheartening loss, however, Bill was always quick to offer a reassuring smile and a positive thought.

He had unparalleled ability. There was never a doubt about his on-air presence and talent in the television industry. When he delivered the sports news of the day, he might as well have been sitting in your living room. He had a fun and easy delivery, never became flustered, and when he made a rare mistake, he was able to laugh at himself, and we would laugh with him.

When he became the voice of the Cowboys, his radio experience was limited, but he adapted to the job with fascinating ease. Over the years, his trademark delivery and signature calls, whether a touchdown or a three-pointer, made his the most recognizable voice in Oklahoma sports.

To Janis, Amanda, the rest of his family, and his countless friends, I want to underscore what a privilege it was to work with Bill. It was even more of a privilege and honor to be his friend.

We will never forget this man who left a part of himself in everything he did.

—EDDIE SUTTON

Tulsa, Oklahoma – 1971

I remember the moment when I first saw Bill. It was 4:58 in the afternoon—a few minutes until the end of my shift at Tulsa's upscale Sipes Grocery. I had been working the cash register since 8:00 a.m. and my feet ached from standing on the hard concrete floor. I wanted to escape the fluorescent lights that seemed particularly harsh that day, go home, get out of my starched uniform, soak in a warm bath, and maybe call a friend.

One more customer and I could close out my line. As I checked the price of the pack of Wrigley's Spearmint gum that a guy about my age laid on the counter, I noticed his blue eyes half hidden behind black horn-rimmed glasses. "He's kinda' cute," I thought. I liked his dimples and there was something about his energy. I noticed the Sipes nametag pinned to his shirt. He was a fellow employee. Why had I never noticed this guy?

I chuckled at his last name—Tietgens. As he paid for the gum and walked off, I thought, "Sure wouldn't want to marry him and get stuck with that name. Always having to spell it."

The next day, Bill was back again, deliberately waiting behind a string of customers, choosing my register to pay for his second gum purchase. It became his habit to pass through my check out line with one pack of gum before he went home each day. We were nice to each other, but did not have a real conversation for weeks. My main concern became his teeth. Surely chewing so much gum would cause them to rot and fall out!

Then, on what seemed to be his 100th purchase of Wrigley's gum, Bill laid his money on the counter and, in a half-stammer, asked, "Do you like baseball?"

I had watched my brother Jim play baseball all my life. Still, my confident response surprised me. "As a matter of fact, I do," I said.

"The Tulsa Oilers are playing Saturday night—wanna' go?" Bill asked, with a burst of optimism.

I was pleasantly surprised at his invitation, it was much better than the usual humdrum, dinner date, and a movie. In a fateful moment, and without hesitation, I answered, "I'd love to!"

"Really?" Bill did a double take, "You sure?"

Ours was a whirlwind romance. Three months later we were engaged and married within a year.

I never dreamed that our love story would tragically end on a cold, wintry day nearly 30 years later in a snow-covered field in rural Colorado.

Boston, Massachusetts – January 27, 2001

I was exhausted after putting in nine hours as a flight attendant for Delta Airlines, and I looked forward to getting to bed early at my apartment near Boston's Logan Airport. As I fought with the stubborn apartment lock, my cell phone rang. "Good, it's Bill," I thought. But it wasn't Bill, it was Nikki Kaehler, our daughter Amanda's best friend and college roommate.

Nikki said, "Janis, an OSU plane is missing. It's all over the news. Two planes made it back from Colorado—one didn't. Have you heard from Bill? I'm trying to reach Amanda."

Nikki's panic was contagious—my heart pounded harder as I hung up to call someone. But who?

I knew Bill was in Colorado to broadcast the Oklahoma State University basketball game. Though we both traveled a lot, we called each other every day. Was that why I had been unable to contact him all afternoon? He worried about me and my dangerous job as a flight attendant. He teased me and said I should get a safe job like his as a television sportscaster and stop flying commercial airlines 75 hours a month.

A dozen thoughts cluttered my mind as my cell phone rang again—this time it was a frantic Amanda. "Mom!" she screamed, "Is it true? Is my Dad dead?" I thought, "Oh no! Nikki has reached Amanda before I could."

I tried to be calm and reassuring. "Let's not jump to conclusions. Wait until we find out if he was even on that plane. Give me a few minutes and I'll make some calls."

Who? How? In my panic, I could not remember the main telephone number to Channel 9, the Oklahoma City television station where Bill worked as sports director for the previous 14 years. I began to tremble and I dialed several wrong numbers before I made the right connection.

A woman answered, "News Nine assignment desk." I said only my name and there was a long pause. Then the woman said, "Kelly, you'd better take this one—it's Janis."

That anonymous voice told me *everything*. In that horrible instant, I knew with icy certainty that it was true. My Bill had died in that plane crash.

After what seemed like an eternity, Kelly Ogle, who happened to be our neighbor and also a friend, picked up the phone. All he said was, "Janis, I am so, so sorry."

I want to be a sports announcer.

BILLY TIETGENS, AGE 8

chapter 1

A MINNESOTA BEGINNING

ill Tietgens was born on July 26, 1952, in Moorhead, Minnesota, at St. Ansgar Hospital. He was christened William Bruce Tietgens after his father, William Edward Tietgens. To avoid confusion, Bill's father became "Bill, Sr." to the world, and young Bill was nicknamed "Billy." Bill, Sr. missed his son's birth, having left for active duty in the Army 22 days prior.

Moorhead is in Clay County, across the Red River from Fargo, North Dakota, where the Tietgens family lived. Bill, Sr.'s parents, Dougald W. "Dietz" Tietgens and Edna Tietgens, and his grandparents, William Tietgens and Euphemia Tietgens, were prominent citizens of Fargo and had been in the farming and laundry/dry cleaning business for decades.

William Edward introduced himself as "Bill Tietgens," to a beautiful Norwegian girl, Carol Ann Vold, at a Fargo party in 1951 and fell in love with her instantly. She had grown up on her family's farm in Lisbon, North Dakota, but after high school relocated to Fargo to find a job.

Bill, Sr.'s mother, Edna, died suddenly of a cerebral hemorrhage in early 1951. Later that year, on November 2, Bill, Sr. and Carol were married.[1] The newlyweds definitely wanted children and it was no time before the doctor announced that Carol was pregnant. Then, the Korean War, raging half a world away, interfered.

Bill, Sr. did not expect to be called to military service because, at age 17, he burned his eyes after spending too much time under a sun lamp. Shortly after, when he tried to enlist in the Navy, he failed the eye test.

In 1950, when North Korea invaded South Korea, hostilities swiftly developed into a war that involved the United States and 19 other

Bill, Sr. and Carol Tietgens on their wedding day in November 1951.

countries. The United States needed to enforce its commitment to South Korea and Bill, Sr. received his draft notice when he and Carol had been married only two months. He passed the Army physical and eye exam with flying colors.

On July 4, Bill, Sr. was shipped overseas to Augsburg, Germany, as a member of Heavy Mortar Company's 102nd Regiment of the 43rd Army Infantry Division, where he received the telegram on July 26, 1952, announcing that he was the father of a six pound eight ounce son. As soon as Bill, Sr. could race to the base telegraph office, he told Carol how happy he was that their new baby was a boy.

LEFT: The telegram announcing Billy's birth.

BELOW: After he was notified that his son had been born thousands of miles away, Bill, Sr. sent this telegram to his beloved wife Carol.

ABOVE: Carol Tietgens with her son, Billy, while his father served in the Army. **RIGHT:** Billy, age one.

Bill, Sr. would not meet his new son, Billy, for 17 months. Overseas telephone calls were too expensive for Private First Class pay, so Bill, Sr. and Carol spoke only once during that time. But, they wrote each other every day, longing for the war to be over so Bill, Sr. could return home and meet his first born son.

During this time, Carol and young Billy lived with her parents, Alvin and Stella Vold, on the family farm, near the small town of Lisbon, North Dakota, about 75 miles southwest of Fargo. Carol cared for the blue-eyed, brown-haired Billy with the help of his loving Nana and Grandpa Vold.

A generation before, Alvin's father, Ole, had been born in Norway and, when he was old enough, followed fellow countrymen to the rich farm-lands in North Dakota. After becoming an American citizen, he shortened the family name from Skjervold to Vold. Ole passed away a few months before Billy was born. Ole's wife, Caroline, was delighted to have a new life to nurture. She gladly helped care for her newest great grandson.[2]

With Bill, Sr. stationed so far away, Carol meticulously recorded Billy's every move in a pink satin baby book. Billy gained 19¹/₂ ounces during his first month and his first outing was to Great Grandma Caroline Vold's farm when he was three weeks old. When Billy was six and a half months old, he said his first word, "Da-Da." Carol wrote Bill, Sr. that his son was already calling him by name, making the distance between Germany and North Dakota seem even farther.[3]

Billy's first birthday—as well as several birthdays to follow—was celebrated at nana and grandpa Vold's farm. Late that night, Carol wrote in the baby book that Bill, Sr. had planned to phone that day, "but the call never came through."[4] Oscar and Almer Vold, Billy's uncles, and their families also helped to celebrate Billy's first birthday.

LEFT: Billy's extended family. Left to right, Nana Stella and Grandpa Alvin Vold, Uncle Oscar Vold, and Aunt Adeline and Uncle Almer Vold. The Severson sisters, Stella and Adeline, married the Vold brothers, Alvin and Almer.

RIGHT: Four generations of Bill's mother's family. Left to right, great grandmother, Caroline Vold; grandfather, Alvin Vold; Billy; and his mother, Carol (Vold) Tietgens.

Billy was finally united with his father in December 1953.

After more than a year on the Vold farm, Carol and Billy moved in with Bill, Sr.'s brother, Clayton, and his wife, Marge, in Fargo. By the time Bill, Sr.'s Army duty was over, Carol and the baby had settled into a tiny apartment in Fargo to await the new father's homecoming.

It was snowing heavily on December 20, 1953, when Bill, Sr. arrived in Fargo. He hailed a taxi toward "home," a strange apartment and a child he had never seen. He was whistling—prompting the taxi driver to ask, "How can you be so happy on such a tough night in the winter?" Bill, Sr. explained, "I have a 17-month-old son

I have never met, a beautiful wife I haven't seen in months, and I can't wait!"

Bill, Sr. arrived at the apartment unannounced. He found Carol and Billy bundled in coats and hats waiting for Clayton and Marge to take them to a Christmas party at the church.

Bill, Sr. rushed to take his son into his arms. Billy resisted the eager "stranger." "I'm your daddy," Bill, Sr. told him. Billy pointed to a picture of Bill, Sr. on the dresser and said, "No, that's daddy!"[5]

Within a few weeks, Bill, Sr. and Billy were best buddies. When spring came, Billy loved to escape the confines of their small apartment and run to his heart's delight with his daddy in nearby Island Park.

For the first few months he was home, Bill, Sr. worked for his uncle delivering laundry to businesses and homes on Broadway Avenue, Fargo's main strip. Occasionally, Billy tagged along with daddy on his route. Bill, Sr. would double-park along the busy street, cut the engine, and carry laundry bundles to his customers. One day, he returned to the truck and noticed the keys missing from the ignition. After Bill, Sr. convinced his son that this was not a good time for a hide and seek game, Billy pointed to the mounds of laundry in the back of the truck. Cars honked and people yelled while Bill Sr. frantically searched for the lost keys, one of those stories that can only seem funny years later![6]

In 1954, Bill, Sr. went to work for Retail Credit Company, a large national credit bureau that forged the lead in a new industry, checking credit for customers who, in the post-war economy, were suddenly buying everything from furniture to cars on credit. Carol was soon expecting their second child and had a big craving for green grapes. She would sit for hours sharing big bowls-full with two-year old Billy, as they watched the World Series on TV—possibly a reason for Bill's later great love for baseball, and also for grapes.

Then, on October 24, 1954, a second son, Scott, was welcomed into the family. Billy was proud of his little brother, and when they were old enough, they became inseparable playmates. The boys enjoyed sledding, ice hockey, cub scouts, and playing little league baseball together.

The Tietgens' family lived the typical Beaver Cleaver life, in that the father worked and the mother stayed home with the children. In this

loving and secure environment, Billy talked early and certainly was not shy. Once, he and his mother were walking in downtown Fargo when the mayor approached. Billy ran up to the mayor, stuck out his hand, and said, "Hello, I'm Billy." The mayor took his hand and replied, "Well, hi there Billy."

When Billy was five, the Tietgens moved to East Grand Forks, Minnesota, where Bill, Sr. worked at the nearby Retail Credit Company office. There,

ABOVE: Even as a toddler, Billy liked to watch television. Little did he or his family know that much of his life would be spent in front of a television camera.

RIGHT: Billy, right, and his little brother Scott, were good friends.

the school system offered kindergarten only from March to May. Just as Carol prepared to enroll Billy, Bill, Sr. was transferred again, this time to St. Paul, Minnesota.

On September 8, 1958, with no kindergarten experience, Billy began first grade—and did very well—at McClellan Elementary School in St. Paul.

St. Paul Sunday

SUNDAY EDITION OF
ST. PAUL, MINN., SUND

TH YEAR—NO. 222   190 PAGES

Billy's photograph on the front page of the *St. Paul Sunday Pioneer Press* on December 5, 1959.

A SASSY CHIHUAHUA looks about in wonderment as her new-found friend, Billie Tietgens, 7, 988 Kilburn, fondles her at the St. Paul Animal shelter on Beulah lane. He was there as the Humane society kicked off its fourth annual Why I Want a Dog for Christmas contest. Each week five puppies are to be awarded boys and girls writing the best letter on the subject. (See story on Page 2).—Staff Photo by D. C. Dornberg

Billy first became a celebrity while at McClellan school. One day the principal called him to the office. Billy thought that he must be in trouble. Instead, the principal explained that someone had spotted him in his new red jacket and green hat and wanted him to pose with a small dog for a Christmas advertisement. Bill, Sr. and Carol were elated a few weeks later when they opened the Sunday paper and saw the picture of Billy standing in front of the St. Paul Animal Shelter—holding a Chihuahua and advertising the town's "I Want a Dog for Christmas" contest.[7]

Billy and Scott loved to watch and imitate the Cisco Kid, their favorite television hero. In 1957, the Tietgens took the boys to the Minnesota State Fair in St. Paul. The highlight of the trip was meeting Duncan Renaldo who portrayed the Cisco Kid and seeing that he really did wear his trademark cowboy outfit with black hat and suit with silver buckles all over.[8]

Billy loved sports and enthusiastically followed the Minnesota Twins baseball club and the Vikings football team. He and Scott passed many afternoons playing catch and bouncing baseballs off the garage wall of the new home that the family had moved into in 1960 at White Bear Lake, a suburb of St. Paul. Bill, Sr. was not happy when he discovered most of the paint was gone from the siding where his sons practiced baseball each afternoon.[9]

In the winter, when it was too frigid to play outside, Billy's parents found him in the basement swinging his baseball bat at a string that hung from the rafters, and doing play-by-play descriptions of any game that existed that day in the head of a young fan. He spent hours making up the games, his voice rising to a fever pitch, penetrating the floorboards to where his mother cooked or sewed upstairs. He was especially loud when he was both the announcer and batter, with the bases loaded, in a crucial, mythical game.

Billy paid close attention to radio and television broadcasts of Twins games. Ray Scott, the radio voice of the Twins and the Green Bay Packers, was his sports casting hero. Billy would imitate Ray Scott, switching to a deep, commanding voice, "On to the Twins' ninth with Killebrew, Battery, Allison, and hopefully Moore."[10] For Billy, it was Ray Scott who brought the nightly verdict on the success or failure of the Twins. Years later, when Bill traveled to Salisbury, North Carolina, to receive one of his eight Oklahoma Sportscaster of the Year awards, he saw Bob Woolf, Ray

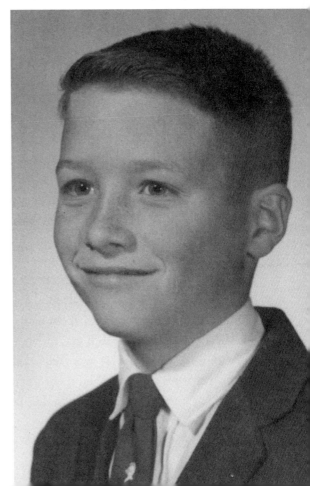

Scott's partner from the Twins' broadcasts in the 1950s. Bill introduced himself and said, "You got me interested in broadcasting." As luck would have it, Ray Scott was in town too for the convention, and Bill was thrilled to be able to have breakfast with both of his childhood broadcasting heroes.[11]

When Billy was eight years old and in the third grade, one night at dinner, he proclaimed, "I want to be a sports announcer." Knowing that most boys that age wanted to be firemen or railroad engineers, his father said, "Well, that will be difficult, but I hope you can."

Baseball became Billy's favorite sport. He avidly began collecting baseball cards and sending for fill-ins off the backs of cereal boxes. He and his brother Scott also collected football cards and comic books, but most of their attention was spent on their cherished stacks of baseball cards. Billy even helped a friend throw his newspaper route in exchange for payment in baseball cards. By adulthood, Bill's baseball card collection grew to more than 3,000.

Bill never cared for cold weather—possibly because of the year he spent as a school crossing guard in the fifth grade at Lakeaires School in White Bear Lake. His mother layered his clothing carefully, but all the bundling in the world would not have fully protected Billy from the 30-degree below zero Minnesota mornings.[12]

On July 30, 1961, the Tietgens were blessed with a third child, a tiny, blue-eyed baby girl they named Paula. Her older brothers were ecstatic to welcome a baby sister into the family, and gave her lots of attention. From the first day, nine-year-old Billy was crazy about her. As soon as Paula could walk, he had her in the driveway tossing baseballs with her. For Bill's entire life, he had a strong sibling relationship with Paula. It's easy to see why. They both shared the same optimistic outlook and dry sense of humor, and they teased each other relentlessly.

Billy and Scott spent several weeks each summer at their Nana and Grandpa Vold's farm in Lisbon, North Dakota. Billy once wrote home, "We have been having lots of fun. We were out in the hay field Monday and Tuesday. How did you like the all-star game? Love, your great son, Billy."[13]

In 1964, Retail Credit Company officials promoted Bill to assistant manager of their Tulsa, Oklahoma office. Bill, Sr. asked for time to think it over before accepting the promotion. However, his boss said, "You have one hour to decide. Go home and discuss it with your wife now."

Bill, Sr. rushed home and talked to Carol. The move would be good for his career but they worried about how it would affect young Billy, who was just entering the seventh grade. They called him at school, and like the team player he always was, Billy said, "That's fine." Bill, Sr. later learned that his son came home from school that day and cried because he did not want to leave his friends. His father remembers, "Even though

Billy loved getting home from school early so he could play baseball with his friends.

he did not want to move, Bill was the kind of child who wanted what was best for the entire family."[14]

Tulsa, Oklahoma, was a long way from family and friends in Minnesota and North Dakota, but it was a change the family hoped would turn out well.

> Bill had an enthusiasm in his voice and the skill to describe the scenery and action with a precision of words.

ELVEN LINDBLAD

chapter 2

MOVING TO OKLAHOMA

*T*ulsa is Oklahoma's second largest city and was named for Tulsey Town, an ancient Creek Indian town in Alabama. After statehood in 1907, Tulsa became known as the Oil Capital of the World, boasting headquarters of many of the nation's largest oil and gas companies.

Oklahoma's oil legacy was evident right away in young Billy's life. He attended seventh grade at William G. Skelly Junior High School in Tulsa, named for a pioneer of the oil patch who had founded Skelly Oil Company.

It didn't take long for Billy to make friends and find other boys his age interested in baseball. One of his early haunts was a really nice baseball park where the Southeast Bears played. Public Service Company of Oklahoma, the local electric company, provided lights and allowed the Bears to use the property, but the parents and volunteers had to meet other expenses and upkeep.

Billy and Scott tried out for teams at the park, and they both earned a position on the Giants team. Most seasons Billy and Scott made the all-star team and Bill, Sr. and Carol hardly missed a game. The boys' biggest fan was their mother, Carol, who used her high school cheerleader training to root for her boys.[1]

The Tietgens' first Christmas in Tulsa was unlike any they had experienced before. It was 70 degrees and considerably warmer than the white Christmases they enjoyed in North Dakota and Minnesota. The Tietgens boys complained of no snow, until after Christmas dinner, Bill, Sr. suggested they go outside and play ball.[2]

Bill and Scott were alike in many ways—they both loved sports and baseball. They were also very different. Scott got involved in rodeo dur-

ing high school and rode bulls until he was kicked in the back. He also played trumpet in the Nathan Hale High School marching band. Bill was more of a talker, a propensity that would greatly help in his future radio and television careers. Scott was more mechanically inclined—he could build or repair anything. Bill was just like his father—they could not "fix" anything.[3]

Religious training was important in the Tietgens household and the family regularly attended Bethany Lutheran Church on East 46th Street in Tulsa, where Bill was confirmed in a special service at the church on October 30, 1966.

Bill had a normal high school career, making decent grades, playing baseball and working at Sipes Grocery Store earning money for college.

One of Bill's most memorable high school evenings was in January, 1970, when the Tietgens men attended the 20th annual Tulsa Oilers Diamond Dinner, known for bringing great baseball personalities to town.

Bill kept the official program on which he had obtained autographs from several stars who were present that night. Oklahoman Johnny Bench was given the *Tulsa World* Award. Mickey Mantle, the most

FAR LEFT: The Southeast Tulsa Giants Team. Billy is third from left on the top row. *Courtesy Larry Cohea.*

LEFT: The three Tietgens children, left to right, Scott, Paula, and Billy.

BELOW: The Tietgens family moved to Tulsa, Oklahoma, in 1964. Left to right, Carol, Paula, Bill, Sr., Billy, and Scott.

RIGHT: Bill's high school senior picture. He was still 17 years old when he graduated in May of 1970.

BELOW: Bill and his sister Paula shared July birthdays and their mother often combined the occasions into one giant family party.

famous baseball player from Oklahoma, received the Hall of Fame Award. Walt "No Neck" Williams won the Pepper Martin Award, and All-Star pitcher Steve Carlton won the Tulsa Alumni Award. Carlton had pitched for the Tulsa Oilers on his way to the major leagues. Casey Stengel, long-time manager of Mantle and the New York Yankees, was also present.[4]

Bill graduated from Nathan Hale High School in May of 1970. The commencement exercises were held at Tulsa's Civic Assembly Center. A portion of a Henry Wadsworth Longfellow poem graced the cover of the commencement program:

> Look not mournfully into the Past. It comes not back again. Wisely improve the Present. It is thine. Go forth to meet the shadowy Future, without fear, and with a manly heart.

Bill began his college education at the University of Tulsa (TU) in September of 1971. TU was originally Henry Kendall College, founded in 1894 by Oklahoma's only congresswoman, Alice Robertson. Kendall Hall housed the TU journalism school, and the campus radio station, KWGS, broadcast from a small one-story brick building located beneath the original radio transmitter tower on the campus.

In his exciting college environment, Bill introduced himself to everyone with a smile and hearty handshake. He often told new friends, such as Elven Lindblad, how his real name was "spelled funny," but was easy to say. Bill always said, "It's Tee, as in a golf tee, and Guns, like you're watching *Gunsmoke* or *Bonanza*."[5]

Students ran the campus radio station. This provided Bill and other aspiring broadcasters an incredible opportunity to practice and sharpen their growing skills. Bill and Larry Burnett teamed up to do the play-by-play and color commentary for TU home basketball games while Lindblad figured running statistics by hand and hosted the halftime interviews.

TU played its basketball games in the 40-year-old Tulsa Fairgrounds Pavilion. Bill, Burnett, and Lindblad sat at a long, wooden table built into an overhang. The booth was a tight squeeze, but gave them a much closer perspective to the court than the tables provided for other media members.

Their close quarters offered a few valuable lessons in emergency broadcasting. Once when Bill was interviewing an NBA scout during halftime, the scout's sweeping arm gesture knocked over a full cup of soda onto the front of Bill's pants. Lindblad remembers the priceless moment, "As the

ABOVE: The KWGS staff in 1972. First row, Bob Lauer. Second row, left to right: Bill Dougan, Russ Cecil, Louise Fink, Ed Dumit, and Lynn Wells. Third row, left to right, Rich Laudon, Ken Terry, Steve Smith, Lee J. Ready, and David Irwin. Fourth row, left to right, Ann Whipple, Vic Bailey, Bill Teegins, Donald Gillmore, Missy Reynolds, John Hart, Randy Kindy, Mike Nichol, Dan Meyers, and Mike Bruckas. Fifth row, left to right, Elven Lindblad, David DeForest, Howard Fogelman, Walters Powers, Leslie Smiley, Richard Dowdell, and Roger Roden. *Courtesy Elven Lindblad.*

RIGHT: Bill, giving the sports report on KWGS. Notice the Elvis Presley sideburns.

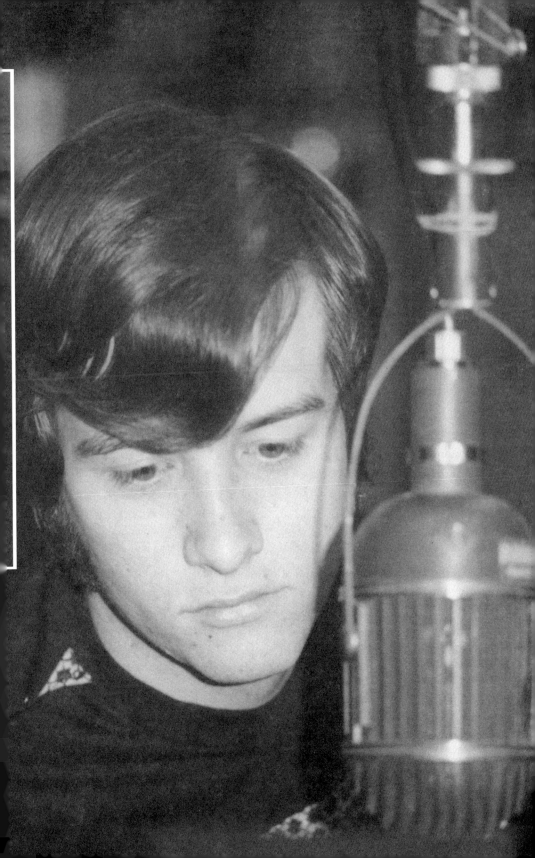

soda and ice spilled onto places where soda and ice are not supposed to be, Bill continued talking without missing a beat. He wrapped up the interview with a couple more questions, threw it back to the station for a public service announcement, and then grabbed a bunch of napkins." Bill dried off his pants, leaned over to Lindblad, and said with a big grin, "Ah, the joys of live radio."

Bill loved broadcasting the games, and Lindblad remembers, "Bill had an enthusiasm in his voice and the skill to describe the scenery and action with a precision of words."[6]

Bill talked non-stop about one subject—baseball. He was the king of baseball trivia. Over the years, he had spent a great deal of time with his enormous baseball card collection memorizing statistics and players' faces. Not only could he recite the birth date and hometown of Twins' pitcher Camilio Pascal, but also the fact that Pascal had begun his professional baseball career playing for the Chickasha, Oklahoma Chicks in the Class D Sooner League in 1960.

Bill liked hanging out with Wayne McCombs, who was also a huge baseball fan. McCombs met Bill in radio announcing class and continually tried to cross Bill up with obscure baseball trivia questions such as, "What was the starting lineup for the 1947 Chicago White Sox?" To everyone's amazement, Bill could "rattle off" the lineup without hesitation.[7]

Bill was often teased about his Minnesota Twins' lack of success, especially in Tulsa, a hotbed of St. Louis Cardinals fans. When Bill was named sports director at KWGS, he proudly tacked a large Twins pennant above the desk in his office.

Bill and McCombs spent a lot of their spare time at Oiler Park, rooting for Tulsa's minor league baseball team. They also followed the success of the TU baseball team that was often nationally ranked in the early 1970s. It was for the Oilers that Bill and McCombs were invited to broadcast their first baseball game, an exhibition affair between the TU squad and the Oilers, the St. Louis farm club.

The two young broadcasters acted like a couple of five-year-old kids on Christmas morning as they scrambled up the stairs of the Oiler Park press box to the radio booth. After the game, Bill turned to McCombs and said, "It won't matter how many other games I ever do, I'll always remember my first game here at Oiler Park."[8]

Bill's childlike enthusiasm for baseball was best demonstrated when the Oilers held their annual media baseball game. Bill, McCombs, and others from KWGS were invited to play on a ragtag team made up of Tulsa-area radio and television personalities pitted against sportswriters of Tulsa's two newspapers, the *Tulsa World* and the *Tulsa Tribune*. Bill donned his well-worn Twins cap and played left field. When he trotted past McCombs at third base, he grinned, "as wide as all outdoors," McCombs said. Then Bill shouted to his friend, "Wow! I can't believe I'm actually going to play a game on a real professional baseball field!"[9]

Bill always made time for Lindblad, McCombs, and younger students to teach them what he knew about the nuances of live broadcasting. The KWGS staff from the early 1970s firmly established themselves in journalism and broadcasting. Burnett eventually became an anchor on ESPN's *SportsCenter*, Richard Dowdell had a long career as a news reporter and anchor at KRMG Radio in Tulsa, and Wayne McCombs became a successful sportswriter, broadcaster, and authored the definitive book on baseball in Tulsa, *Let's Goooooooo Tulsa!* Lindblad has enjoyed a 30-year career in sports production.[10]

As one would expect, when college guys got together, the conversation often segued from broadcasting and sports, to women. McCombs remembers, "Many in our group talked about their dates and bragged about how many phone numbers they had. But Bill was not that way."[11]

Bill had a new girl he had met at Sipes Grocery store…and that's where I come into the story.

> We had a deep love.
> We were soul mates.
>
> **JANIS TEEGINS**

chapter 3

LOVE FOR A LIFETIME

I was born Janis Marie Gibson in Wichita, Kansas, on January 21, 1953. I had a wonderful childhood with my parents, Raymond Gibson and Nanette Thompson Gibson, and with my brother, Jim, who was two years older than me.

My family is not known for long courtships. On March 1, 1950, after dating only three weeks, my parents secretly eloped to Amarillo, Texas. The justice of the peace married mom and dad after mom, only 16 years old, fudged about her age.

Dad was employed as a mechanic for Boeing in Wichita, a trade he learned serving as a Sea Bee in the United States Navy shortly after World War II. In 1957, dad went to work as a mechanic for American Airlines in Tulsa, after training at Spartan School of Aeronautics.

My maternal grandfather, Philo B. Thompson, couldn't say much about my parents eloping. In 1886, at age eight, Grandpa came with his parents to Indian Territory. Later he met Eula Mae Herndon in a five and dime store in Marlow. He fell in love immediately and they were soon married. Philo and Eula Mae farmed and raised cotton outside Rush Springs, Oklahoma, for nearly 30 years.

During World War II, they moved to Oklahoma City, where Philo worked at Tinker Air Field. They raised 10 children, and Nanette, being next to the youngest in the large and noisy brood, learned early to know what she wanted and to step forward to claim it.

My father's parents were equally as determined and sure of their places in life. His mother, Geneva Diemer Gibson, was a tiny woman with a strong will, and a heart of gold, who spent much of her life as an ordained Pentecostal evangelist. She ran feeding programs for the

Janis' family in 1954. From top left, Janis' father, Raymond Gibson, her mother, Nanette "Nan" Thompson Gibson, her big brother Jim, and Janis.

poor and preached in churches and tent revivals in Tulsa and Oklahoma City. While growing up, my brother Jim and I loved to stay with Granny Geneva on weekends and help her conduct church and Sunday school.

One of our favorite memories of Granny Geneva is her

ABOVE: Left to right, Janis' grandfather, Philo Thompson, with sons, Acey, Fred, Max, and Gerald.

standing in her little yellow kitchen after her exuberant preaching was done for the day, with her high heels kicked off, cooking us delicious ham and beans, fried potatoes, and corn bread while she told us stories about our father's boyhood. We called this a meal "fit for a king," and Granny Geneva made us feel every bit like the king's only children.

Geneva had married James McFarland Gibson, but then thought better of that decision and, in a time when divorce was nearly unheard of, divorced my grandfather when my dad was still a young boy.

Grandpa Jim, as my brother and I called him, was a tall, handsome man with a deep, booming voice we loved. He later married Katherine Tisdale, and together they lovingly raised six children. Grandpa Jim was a top-notch car salesman. Jim and I often visited him and his second family at their home near Fayetteville, Arkansas.

LEFT: Janis' grandfather and grandmother, Philo and Eula Mae Thompson.

RIGHT: Janis' paternal grandmother, Geneva Diemer Gibson, with Jim and Janis in January of 1957.

BELOW: Janis' father snapped this picture of Janis and Jim posing with their mother on family vacation in Santa Monica, California, in October of 1957.

Janis at age one.

Grandpa Jim raised cocker spaniels and he surprised me one Christmas with a blonde puppy we named "Blondie." She was part of our lives for 17 years.

I graduated from Tulsa's East Central High School in 1971 and began my studies at Tulsa Junior College. I also worked part-time as a checker at Sipes Grocery Store, which is no longer in business. Sipes was a classy, upscale establishment that required employees to maintain a neat appearance and to give customers friendly, competent, and polite service at all times.

On a June day in the summer of 1971, I was standing in the back room at Sipe's waiting for the rusty time clock to click one more noisy second to signal the official start of my shift. All at once, a guy rushed past me yelling four-letter words and shouting, "I haven't even been here two minutes and already they're already screaming my name over the intercom!" He seemed surprised to see me, and mumbled something under his breath like, "Sorry, didn't see you there."

I was a new employee and, being half embarrassed for the guy, barely looked at him. I must have been somewhat taken with him

Jim and Janis, growing up in Tulsa in 1957.

The 1965 Hamilton Junior High School football queen and her court. Left to right, Vickie Miller, queen Linda Trine, and Janis.

though, because I remember that I jumped straight up when the clock ticked 8:00 a.m., and quickly punched in my time card so I could get out of the office and begin my day.

Every day after that, Bill came through my register to buy gum—lots of Wrigley's spearmint gum! He didn't ever say much, certainly nothing spectacular, but he was always nice and I thought he was very cute. I wondered how cute he'd be when his beautiful straight teeth rotted and fell out from chewing all that gum.

My first recollection of hearing Bill call a game was when our assistant store manager, Don Peeveyhouse, taped the microphone open on the Sipe's intercom system and sat a transistor radio next to it so that the employees and shoppers could listen to University of Tulsa basketball on game days.

During lulls in business at my station as a check out clerk, I loved listening to the games. And I loved listening to the voice of the announcer.

"Man, who is that guy?" I asked someone nearby during the first game day that I worked. "I've never heard anyone talk that fast, but I can totally see the action that he's describing."

"That's Bill Tietgens, the boy who buys all that gum from you," my neighboring cashier told me, laughing like she already knew a secret.

"Wow," I thought, "I have something in common with that darling boy; we both love sports."

Everyone in my family followed sports. As a teenager, I was always hanging around my brother Jim, bugging him to play catch with me or getting him to teach me how to kick the football. Mom coached my fast pitch softball team in grade school. Dad was a die-hard OU football fan, and Jim played sports all through school. We'd all sit around on weekends and watch baseball, football, tennis, or any sport that was televised. In junior high, I roller-skated competitively, and my parents drove me to skating meets in a five state region.

Earlier in this story, you read how Bill stopped simply buying gum and finally asked me out to the Tulsa Oilers game. We had such a wonderful time. Bill was happy that I knew how the game was played. It left him free to talk in circles about how he wanted to be a sportscaster and how baseball was his favorite sport. I heard about his huge collection of cards, which he promised to show me, surely an indication that he liked me. I remember thinking, "God, please let him ask me out again."

Both Bill and I had been dating other people before going to the Oilers game. However, after our first date, we had little time for anyone else. We became great friends and constant companions. In between classes at TU, he worked part-time at KWGS, the student radio station on campus. He also worked a few hours a day at KFMJ Radio, where he hosted a daily music show, reported news and sports, and recorded commercials. It was a small broadcasting operation at which disc jockeys were expected to wear several hats. I was happy that he continued to work at Sipes as his main job, but his long hours at the radio stations helped him get needed experience for the sportscasting job that he already knew he would someday have.

Bill often took me to KWGS with him. We talked and teased during the songs he played in the station's classical music format. There was a bit of rebel in Bill because he would occasionally slip in a Rolling Stones or Leon Russell record, ruffling the feathers of listeners and catching me by surprise, making me laugh every time.

We both enjoyed movies and planned some of our first dates around new releases. A few movies that we enjoyed together were, "The

From their first date, Bill and Janis spent a lot of time at their parents' homes and attended every imaginable kind of sporting event.

Graduate," "Love Story," "Butch Cassidy and the Sundance Kid," and "Funny Girl."

I'll never forget the first time Bill came to my house to meet my parents. I wasn't too worried about my dad—except for the fact that he was really strict and not overly friendly to any of my dates. Mom, on the other hand, was a character and always had something up her sleeve. She reminded me a lot of Lucille Ball, on "I Love Lucy," and she had about as many shenanigans.

Mom had just purchased a new couch for the living room. Bill, being polite, told her how much he liked the couch. "Well, the salesman said if I decide that I don't like it for any reason, he'll come pick it up and exchange it," she bragged.

A few days later, when Bill came to pick me up to go to a movie, there was a different couch in the living room. "What happened to the other couch, Nan?" he asked. "Well, Bill, they said that if I didn't like it, they'd bring me a new one. So here it is," she said.

The same scene—with at least two or three more sofas—occurred during the next month. The whole family was relieved when Mom finally settled on the couch she wanted. Frankly, I didn't care what sofa we had—I just worried that Bill would think my mom was terribly goofy. That concern of mine made me realize that I liked Bill in a different way from the way I'd liked guys before. But from the start, he joined in Mom's fun and I found that I enjoyed seeing the two of them together. He was always curious to see what she'd come up with next.

A couple of days before Christmas, Dad brought Mom's beautifully store wrapped present home and purposely placed it in the top of the living room closet, admonishing her, "Don't open this package until Christmas Day!" The second that dad left to run an errand, Bill looked shocked, but definitely intrigued, as Mom carefully climbed onto a chair and retrieved her present. She'd untied the ribbons, meticulously pulled the tape loose without even tearing the foil paper, unwrapped the present, showed Bill and me her pretty new sweater, and rewrapped it to its exact original state. Dad never knew about the incident, but Bill got a big kick out of it.

On another occasion, Mom decided that she wanted to sell the house—but Dad was dead set against it. Mom and her best friend, who lived across the street, made a "For Sale by Owner" sign and hammered it into the ground in the front yard every day the second that dad left for work. Mom always removed the sign just before Dad drove into the drive. I'm not sure what she would have done if she'd sold the house, but after a while she stopped the daily routine and everyone forgot about her desire to pack up and take her sofa, pretty sweater, and other treasures to a different house. My parents lived in that same house quite happily for another 10 years.

Following my family's tradition of short courtships, Bill I and knew we were in love, and after dating for only three months, wanted to get married. However, we also knew that our parents would think we were too young. I was only 19—Bill was 20, so we got engaged and thought we were keeping it a big secret.

Our attraction to each other, long conversations, and teasing looks must have given us away though because Mr. Parks, the Sipe's store manager, walked up to us one day and said, "You're such a cute couple. You two should should just go ahead and get married."

Bill and I worked with some real characters at Sipes. Bucky Conger, who surely had 90 lives, was one of them. He looked and acted like Andy Kaufman who starred in the sitcom, "Taxi." We had more laughs at Bucky's antics. The most memorable was the day when he tripped over a ladder in the aisle and hurt his foot. In a fit of anger, he carried the metal ladder to the box-crushing machine and jammed it in. We had never heard such loud, high pitched, screeching noises in our high-class grocery store before, as the box-crusher tried to rise to the occasion to grind a long metal ladder. Bucky was in big trouble with the boss, but somehow his job was spared and we had many more of Bucky's pranks to look forward to.

Finally, Bill and I announced our engagement and set a wedding date nine months off—August 25, 1973. We believed that that much time would allow us to get to know each other perfectly and would help us make sure we wanted to spend the rest of our lives together.

Religion could have been a dividing issue for us. I was a member of East Tulsa Christian Church and Bill and his family attended Bethany Lutheran Church. I was open to attending his church, though, especially after meeting Bill's pastor, the Reverend Herbert Meyer, who informed us that he would perform the marriage only after we completed six weeks of marriage counseling.

Those sessions were helpful and laid a strong foundation for our faith, our marriage, and for our strong commitment to each other. I'm still glad that we went through the counseling as it helped us get off on the right foot, basing our marriage on God, family, and trust. Looking back, I think that that threefold focus is what made our marriage so good—and it was so good. For all the years that Bill and I were together, it seemed like a continual date.

I'll never forget the day we picked out my engagement ring and took it to show Bill's mother. When I held out my hand, boasting the new solitaire diamond, Carol burst into tears. "Uh, oh!" I thought, "Not even married yet, and my future mother-in-law doesn't like me!" As it turned out, that wasn't the case at all. Carol was happy for us, but the thought of her firstborn son, the baby she spent raising the first year and a half on her own, was getting married.

Bill turned 21 years old the month before our wedding. His father used the occasion to write Bill a letter containing the last advice he felt he could give before Bill "came of age." Bill, Sr. wrote:

Bill and Janis with his mother, Carol.

I'm so happy for you that you will have Janis for your wife. I know she will be a good wife and we all love her very much. My prayer for you is that she will make you as happy as your mother has made me.

Bill, keep God first in your life, and there will never be any problems that are too big to handle. Don't just depend on yourself, but put your faith in God and he will work it out. Also, Bill, don't take things too seriously, but try and always keep a good sense of humor…In other words, have patience.

One more bit of advice…set your goals high. You have a lot of ability, a good personality, and most important of all, your Tietgens smile. Aim high Bill and you will make it.

With all my love,
Dad

Our wedding day—a typically hot August day in Tulsa—finally came. The outside temperature was more than 100 degrees, and the air conditioning was not working properly in the bride's dressing room at Bethany Lutheran Church. I was more than warm when, at 8:00 p.m. sharp, I finally escaped the room and walked down the aisle with my dad.

Just three weeks before the ceremony, Bill's parents had been transferred to Amarillo, Texas, so they had to make a quick return to Tulsa for the event. Other than the heat getting to the wedding cake and cracking it straight down the middle, and me being hot and sweaty while getting ready, it was a lovely wedding. We had many friends and family members there to share in our new beginning.

I give full credit to Bill's brother, Scott, for the biggest problems on our wedding day. After a reception in the church fellowship hall, we made a dash for Bill's red car which was properly covered with shaving cream, toilet paper, and shoe polish. "Just Married" graffiti covered the windows and the sides of the car. Scott went so far as to rub smelly sardines on the car's door handles for a nice surprise to start us off right.

It was beginning to get dark and we did not notice that the car was hiked up in the back. Scott had used two small jacks to lift the car's back tires off the ground. Bill started the car, threw it into reverse, and we went…nowhere. He gunned the engine as I snapped, "Well, put it in gear."

ABOVE: Bill and Janis were married on August 25, 1973—a storybook, romantic marriage and a partnership.

RIGHT: Janis' big day, August 25, 1973, when she became Bill's bride. She knew they were off to a good start because they were already best friends.

"It's in gear; it just won't go!" he yelled. It was our first fight, but it quickly ended when Scott admitted his prank and let down the car so we could roll safely away.

Later that night, after opening our suitcases, we found mounds of rice layered between our clothes, especially our underwear. Scott and his cohorts must have used five boxes of Uncle Ben's, I guess because it was cheap!

We had planned to stay our first night at the Hilton Hotel, just a block from the church. After our gear shift tiff, as we finally drove away, Bill did a good job of blocking our view when he turned on the windshield wipers and caused the shaving cream to smear and fly everywhere. With tin cans clacking, we drove around for a while, making sure that no one was following us. We endured the honks and yells from dozens of motorists until we finally decided to stop at a car wash and, in our wedding finery, remove the "gunk" placed there by our very humorous friends and family.

After checking in at the hotel, thinking we'd been so well hidden, we discovered that Bill's Aunt Janice and Uncle Dick Hoerber had left a bottle of champagne in our room with a note attached, "Hit a home run, Bill." From that moment on, I knew that sports would play a giant role in our lives.

We didn't have a lot of extra money and so we decided to have an inexpensive honeymoon at Western Hills Lodge near Grand Lake in northeast Oklahoma. Our plan was to begin saving immediately to buy a home that we both wanted. We shared beautiful sunsets on the lake, and we took advantage of the nice amenities at the lodge, which included tennis, swimming, and, of course, televised baseball games.

One of Bill's high school buddies, Jim Freeman, was pitching for the Atlanta Braves and Bill was excited about watching him on television. I enjoyed sitting through the game too because he loved sports, and, well— I loved him.

After the honeymoon, Bill and I returned to Tulsa to the real world of earning a living and everyday married life. I continued to work at Sipes, and Bill was assistant news director at KRAV-FM Radio. He broadcast five-minute newscasts several times a day and was a field reporter, covering happenings at city hall and other events. He also produced weekly news specials.

Bob Bethel was news director at KRAV and was a successful Tulsa radio personality as well as being an amateur theater actor. He later became known for his portrayal of *Scrooge* in "A Christmas Carol," and as *Eddie* in "Eddie and The Electics," a 1950s rock and roll show that played at the Brook Theatre on Peoria. Even though Bob was Bill's boss, they became good friends and had many laughs and fun times together.

Bob kept a jar of peanut butter, a loaf of bread, and a knife in his desk. Bill took advantage of the food cache and started eating like crazy when we were first married. He ate peanut butter sandwiches, washed them down with a regular Coke at work, and then stopped on his way home and bought chocolate milk and donuts. When he began to develop a "tire" around his waist, he cut back.

On Saturdays, Bill worked from 6:00 p.m. to midnight at KRAV. I often tagged along with him on Saturday nights to keep him company. Too excited to be together after our separate busy days, during the early part of Bill's evening shift, we'd lose ourselves in conversation and Bill would often forget to cue up the next record. When the song ended, and there was nothing but dead air, loud, screaming alarms would sound and Bill would have to scramble to the turntable in a panic to cue up the next record. Meanwhile, I would collapse in giggles.

Management frowned on dead air, because if a client who'd bought advertising time heard it, they might cancel their account. That was long before the days of automation and compact discs that practically eliminate the chance of that happening.

After a couple of hours of conversation, I'd get tired and push two chairs together and try to get comfortable enough to sleep until it was time for us to pack up and drive home to our little apartment.

Bill's pay at KRAV was at the low end of the scale. In fact, I made more at Sipes than Bill did at his radio job. However, we both knew that broadcasting was Bill's niche and we accepted the fact that he'd have to pay his dues, just like everyone else, to get to his ultimate goal of being a sportscaster. Bill was very aware of the stories of his sportscaster heroes, who had all started small and worked their way up the ladder, rung by dreary rung.

Like any other young newlywed couple, we had our ups and downs. But for the most part, even from the very beginning, we were a good fit, incredibly happy, and always anxious to be with each other, to share our stories, our days—though we couldn't have known it then, we were not to get as many days as we hoped.

What's the matter with those people in Texas? Can't they spell Tietgens?

**DIETZ TIETGENS,
BILL'S GRANDFATHER**

chapter 4

OFF TO WEST TEXAS

ill, Sr. was very proud of all his children and took delight in having a namesake. In Amarillo, where Bill, Sr.'s job took him, he constantly bragged to his friends about his son, Bill, who was in broadcasting, and his son Scott, who worked at Vinson Supply Company. Bill Hays was one of Bill, Sr.'s bowling buddies who also owned a local advertising agency. Hays asked Bill, Sr. if he could get an audition tape of Bill. When Hays heard Bill, he said, "Well, he's got a great voice. There may be an opportunity for him in this market."[1]

Two weeks later, Bill and I happened to be visiting his parents when Hays called with news that Bill was invited to read for a screen test for a news reporter position at KFDA-TV, channel 10, the CBS affiliate in Amarillo, Texas. Bill had only packed blue jeans and sweatshirts for the relaxing weekend we had looked forward to with his parents. Hays said the apparel would not matter and marched Bill right in and introduced him to Ron Slover, the news director at the station. Bill had been nervous beforehand and practiced for the interview by reading the newspaper aloud in front of a mirror.[2]

After Bill completed the screen test, he told his father, "I think I got the job, but they want me to spell my name differently for television." The KFDA management complained that Tietgens was a hard name to spell and even worse to pronounce. They had suggested spelling it TEEGINS instead so people could easily identify it. Bill's father understood but said, "I hope you don't permanently change the spelling of our name, son."

Bill had no intention of changing it officially but, for television, that's how, and when Bill Tietgens became "Bill Teegins." When Bill's grandfather, Dietz Tietgens, heard the news in North Dakota, he was less understanding. He called Bill, Sr. and asked, "What's the matter with those people in Texas? Can't they spell Tietgens?[3]

Bill was right—his screen test was a success and he he got the job as a general assignment news reporter for KFDA-TV. We packed up and moved to Amarillo on March 1, 1975, which also happened to be my parents 25th wedding anniversary. I could tell that they were upset, simply because they didn't want us to move away from Tulsa. Nevertheless, I think deep down they understood and they wished us much luck as we pulled out, trailing after the moving van, our car loaded with plants and plans for our new home. Tulsa was a hard market to break into television without any experience, and Amarillo provided Bill the opportunity to get that experience.

Bill never really liked reporting general news—partly because he thought so many of the news stories were depressing. Mostly, though, it was because he had a burning in his soul—since he was eight years old, he had wanted to be talking sports, he wanted to be a sportscaster. Still, as the new kid on the block at KFDA, he anchored the noon news on weekdays. On the weekend, he had the 6:00 and 10:00 p.m. time slot. He did a good job too.

We had been in Amarillo only one week when Bill's grandfather, Alvin Vold, died in North Dakota. Alvin had suffered from cancer for more than ten years. Bill was broken hearted that he could not get off to attend the funeral, but his family understood.

Bill's hard work and early loyalty paid off. Just three months after Bill began at KFDA, at age 22, he was promoted to producer, and anchored the 6:00 and 10:00 p.m. newscasts. With the goal that he might soon become a sportscaster, he worked hard in the news business. He was on the job 10 hours a day, six days a week, shooting and editing his own video, going anywhere there was a story, telling it the very best way he could.

I had a daytime job as a new accounts representative at American National Bank in downtown Amarillo. With opposite hours, Bill and I did not see each other very much. In order to make time together, I occasionally rode with him in his news car, listening to the police scanners for any late breaking stories that might be unfolding, such as a fire, robbery, or a kidnapping. We chased ambulances to hospitals, trying to get video of the aftermath of automobile accidents, or a shooting. Together, we looked for any story that could make his newscasts more interesting.

ABOVE: Bill and his Channel 10 mobile news unit in Amarillo, 1975. Bill landed the job as general assignment news reporter for the CBS affiliate.

LEFT: Bill's grandmother, Stella Vold, center, visiting Bill and Janis in Amarillo. This photograph was taken in 1976.

Bill and Janis at Bill's parents' home in Amarillo, Texas, in 1975.

Continuing to work as a news anchor was a challenge—in more than one way. The camera crew at KFDA, with time on their hands and always looking for a little fun in their day, once tried to break Bill up by taping a centerfold from *Playboy* Magazine to the front of the camera as he tried to deliver a newscast. Every time Bill looked up from his copy toward the camera, he couldn't keep from snickering, even during serious stories. Somehow, even with the distraction, he made it through the newscast without completely bursting into laughter. I'm sure the people watching from home had no idea what was making Bill almost laugh.

Shortly after we moved to Amarillo, Bill's brother, Scott, made a startling discovery in the family's attic—he found Bill's huge collection of baseball cards that had been lost for a couple of years. Bill was as excited as a kid eating his first ice cream cone. He brought the cards home, spread them out around him all over the carpet, whispering comments and thoughts, like they were his long lost friends. Then we began a nightly trivia game—that is, Bill began the nightly trivia game. I was only the event's announcer. Bill had spent so much time with the cards while growing up, he had committed to memory most of the statistics contained on the backs of the cards, minute details he was now prepared to impress me with—for even the most obscure players.

He would have me hold up a card and place my hand over the player's name. Then he'd tell me not only the name of the player, but his position, team, any former team, and incredibly detailed statistics. It was impressive—but became boring to me fairly quickly, especially since he hardly ever missed a question. After a couple of years of nightly baseball trivia, I said, "Sorry sweetie—please take these to work."

Bill religiously read *The Sporting News*, his source for many statistics and interesting stories about sports stars. He didn't dare throw away any past issue, so the clutter in our storage closet, and then our attic, and finally a few stacks even drifting into our bedroom, began to take on the look of a newspaper warehouse. It would be 20 years before I convinced him to stop saving newspapers that neither he, nor anyone else, would ever read again.

Another of Bill's favorite pastimes, that he continued in the early years of our marriage, was to read a big thick annual baseball encyclopedia, a publication that contains every statistic known to baseball, including facts about some player who only batted one time in the major leagues. Night after night, the bedside light burned on

Bill and Debbie Reeves were the news anchors on KFDA-TV in Amarillo, Texas, in 1976.

LEFT: Bill tackling the tires portion of an obstacle course in a KAMR-TV promotion and fundraiser for the Amarillo Olympic Fund.

BELOW: Bill and Janis, after a visit to the local Olan Mills studio. Notice Janis' bouffant hairdo and Bill's very "eighties" coat and vest.

RIGHT: Bill, relaxing between shots on a sports assignment for KAMR-TV in 1978.

while Bill read the encyclopedia and consumed mountains of baseball information. You could say that my ability to sleep through about anything is one of the reasons he was nearly "unstumpable" on any baseball-related trivia question.

After working at KFDA for 17 months, Bill grew discouraged thinking he would never become a sportscaster for the station. Regular news was getting him down. He quit and went to work as a salesman for an electrical supply company in Amarillo. His plans were to travel Oklahoma, Texas, and New Mexico for the company as an outside salesman. When I think back about this, it makes me laugh. Remember the family joke? Bill was about the least mechanically inclined person I had ever met and he certainly knew nothing about electrical supplies. Fortunately, for his future fans, he lasted as an electrical supply salesman only three months.

In November of 1976, Bill got a break—he landed a job as assistant sports director at another Amarillo television station, KAMR-TV. He loved his sports job so much more than being a newsman.

Bill on the set at KAMR-TV in 1980. Janis ironed his shirts and tried to make sure his ties always matched his suit.

The station hired a news consultant who wanted Bill to have more exposure in the market. They created a "sports challenge" in which Bill would compete against athletes in their sport of expertise. Bill's Sports Challenges ranged from riding bulls, to para sailing, wind surfing, and ice hockey. Some of the challenges were dangerous. I made it clear to Bill that he could do what he needed to do, but I didn't want to see or hear about any of the risky ones.

On June 1, 1978, to both of our delights, Bill became sports director at KAMR-TV, where he anchored the 6:00 and 10:00 p.m. sports. He continued to shoot much of his own video for the sportscasts, and he especially liked covering the Gold Sox, Amarillo's baseball team in the Texas League

Even though Bill was extremely happy in his KAMR sports job, he was always on the lookout for any position that might open in bigger markets, hoping to better himself and eventually move on and up.

Bill and I bought our first home in Amarillo just in time for our daughter, Amanda Leigh, to be born on October 7, 1978. Of course, my intense labor pains began just as Bill was due to report his 10:00 p.m.

sportscast. I was at Bill's parents' house, and his mother, Carol, assured me that, after giving birth to three children, she knew exactly when it would be time to go to the hospital. Bill's little sister, Paula, who was an annoying teenager at that time, sat on the bed laughing at me and asking, "Does it really hurt that much?" Years later, Paula received her payback by having two children of her own, two nieces whom I adore.

The second that Bill got off the air, his father called him and told him it was time to drive me to the hospital and have our baby. Bill quickly switched gears and drove home to pick up my suitcase that I'd been packing for weeks. However, I had never zipped it up, and in his rush to get me to the hospital, Bill grabbed the suitcase and scattered the carefully thought out, neatly stacked contents all around the room. He hurriedly threw everything back in, and picked me up at his parents' house and started driving toward the hospital.

Janis' parents with her three months before Amanda was born. The word "BABY" and the arrow on Janis' shirt announced her condition to anyone she met.

We had taken a trial run a few weeks before, at the suggestion of one of our instructors in the baby classes. Bill had done just fine then, telling me about some ball game, no doubt. This was different. Poor Bill was a nervous wreck. On the way to the hospital, he ran over a center median, and I was pretty sure I would have our baby at that very moment. When we finally got to the hospital, he let me off at the wrong door, then zoomed off to find a parking spot. I heard him squeal the tires as he rounded a corner. He slammed into the spot while I was making my way the 30 or so yards to the door, the one Bill was able to find two weeks before. By this time, as I finally entered the hospital, I was bent over in great pain, and quite far along in my labor.

All the effort was worth it when Amanda was born at 2:19 a.m. She was an adorable little red head and weighed six pounds seven ounces. Bill had considered going into the delivery room with me, but after the circus-like trip to the hospital, and with his squeamish stomach, I'm positive that he made the right call to sit out this event in the waiting room.

I think Bill had secretly hoped for a boy, but the moment he saw his little girl, bonding began. He was the best father I'd ever seen—immediately Amanda was nuts about her dad. When Amanda was old enough,

ABOVE: Amanda was baptized at the Beautiful Savior Lutheran Church in Amarillo on February 4, 1979.

LEFT: Bill and Amanda, called "Mandy," bonded from the first time he held her.

she would toddle up to the television set while Bill was on the air, say "Da," and smear the screen with baby kisses. I used a lot of Windex in those days. Kleenex, too—when she would cry because her "screen-daddy," no matter how many kisses she gave him, would never kiss her back.

ABOVE: Bill and his little girl. As soon as she could talk, she called him "Da." Bill called her "Mamie," because that is how Amanda said her own name. Later, she became Mandy to the family.

RIGHT: Amanda was the joy of the Tietgens' lives. Whether watching her daddy on television or swinging with Janis outside, she was a happy baby.

Amanda loved playing dress up, using Janis' makeup and hair rollers. She also loved waiting for her daddy to come home and notice.

We all enjoyed being with Bill's family. Besides his parents, Bill's brother, Scott, and his wife, Audrey, and their daughter, Kati, and son, Clifton; and Bill and Scott's sister, Paula, and her husband, David, also lived in Amarillo. We had many large family gatherings and played a lot of golf and tennis together. On several occasions, the entire group drove five hours to Red River, New Mexico, or to other destinations in the New Mexico mountains to relax, fish, ski, and just enjoy each other's company during several days of vacation.

> *Teegins will be popular wherever he goes.*
>
> **A NEWSPAPER COLUMNIST IN AMARILLO, TEXAS**

chapter 5

BACK HOME

*I*n 1980, Bill interviewed for the sports anchor position at KTUL-TV, Channel 8 in Tulsa, Oklahoma. I was hopeful he would take the job, so that we could move back home and give my parents the chance to enjoy Amanda, their first and only grandchild at that time. The negotiations between Bill and Channel 8's management did not work out and Bill continued looking for a better fit in a market larger than Amarillo.

A year later, friends in Tulsa informed Bill that the sports anchor job at CBS affiliate KOTV, Channel 6 was open because controversial sportscaster, Ken Broo, had left the station for a new position in Tampa, Florida. This time, Bill applied and was quickly hired.

As we sold our home and prepared to return to Tulsa, the local newspaper in Amarillo applauded Bill's six years in the market. One columnist wrote, "Teegins has made a lot of friends in the Texas Panhandle, and he will do well anywhere he goes."[1]

There was both a good and bad side to the move back home to Tulsa. We were sad to leave Bill's parents, his brother and sister, and their families, but; in the same breath, we were excited to return to my roots, to my parents, and to where we had fallen in love and begun this life's journey. Best of all, we still had many friends in Tulsa, and we knew it would be a great place to raise Amanda.

While growing up in Tulsa, Bill's dream had been to someday work at KOTV along side his broadcasting hero, Clayton Vaughn, who had worked in broadcast journalism for 23 years. Clayton's co-anchor on the 5:00 and 10:00 p.m. newscasts was Bob Losure, a well-respected Tulsa native with 11 years of sound experience. Rounding out the team

LEFT: Bill loved Woodward Park, the Tulsa Rose Garden, and to just "take in" Tulsa and the beautiful skyline.

BELOW: The KOTV-6 News team. News co-anchors Bob Losure and Clayton Vaughn; Meteorologist Jim Giles; and Sports Director, Bill Teegins. *Courtesy KOTV.*

Bob Losure Clayton Vaughn Jim Giles Bill Teegins

Eyewitness News 6

was weatherman, Jim Giles, a 26-year veteran with a master's of meteorology degree from the University of Oklahoma.

Bill's closest friend at KOTV became Bob Losure, who was single and often ate dinner alone. One night, after the 6:00 p.m. news, Bill brought Bob to our house unexpectedly, and asked if he could eat dinner with us. "That's great, but we're having leftover Sloppy Joes," I warned. Bob said, that that would be fine, and later, he even thanked me live, during the 10:00 p.m. newscast for "the best Sloppy Joe's he'd ever eaten." I caught a lot of ribbing at church the next Sunday about how I served Sloppy Joe's whenever I had people over for dinner.

In the Tulsa market, Bill's opposition was stellar. Chris Lincoln, Becky Dixon, and Bob Carpenter made up the sports broadcast team at KTUL-TV, Channel 8. Jerry Webber, the sportscaster of KJRH-TV, Channel 2, had been around for years, and was also very popular. However, Bill had staying power and was determined to make his mark in the Tulsa sports arena as quickly as possible. A short time later, Chris left to broadcast thoroughbred horse racing, Bob opted to broadcast the Texas Rangers games and ended up at ESPN, and Becky joined ABC. Jerry eventually switched from sports to news anchor at KJRH, Channel 2.

While at KOTV, Bill became an elector in the annual balloting for the winner of the Heisman Trophy, which recognizes the nation's outstanding college football player, an award from the Downtown Athletic Club of New York City. As always, Bill did his homework. He reviewed the leading candidates' weekly performances, comparing the top players and statistics from each game. Later in the season, he bounced his ideas off colleagues at work and with friends who shared his love for sports. It was a big deal for him when he made his final choice, completed the Heisman ballot, and mailed it back to New York City.

Bill tried to do his best in everything—even fantasy baseball. I always secretly liked this about him. He, Wayne McCombs, Elven Lindblad, and other friends jumped into Tulsa's first fantasy baseball league, the Galaxy League.

"Bill was prudent in selecting the best possible players at each position but it was obvious that when he opened the draft bidding on a Minnesota Twins player, it was wise for us not to try taking that player from him."[2] Elven said.

Bill took his role as a fantasy team owner seriously, with the power to buy, sell, or to trade real major league players on Galaxy League teams with nonsensical nicknames such as the Elves, Whippets, Gladiators, and Visitors. Bill's team was the Vegetables. Wayne remembers that Bill chose the name because when he was a child he had seen a roadside marker, "Bill's Vegetables," and the name had stuck with him.[3]

One night, Wayne watched Bill's sportscast and noticed there was a pattern to the video highlights of that day's baseball games—Bill had chosen highlights involving only players from his fantasy team. One film clip showed a player drawing a base on balls— a walk. *This* was an action highlight? Wayne called Bill at work the next day and they both roared with laughter.[4]

Bill sounded like a real owner when asked about his fantasy team. He'd say something like, "My team is so awful, and my hitters can't hit worth a lick. My starting pitchers give up so many home runs and my relievers start fires instead of putting them out. My team stinks. I oughta' trade every one of those bums."[5]

Bill was rarely sick, but one late night, after he'd been laid up on the couch under blankets with Kleenexes scattered all around him all day, it came time for the Galaxy League pre-season draft. Team owners met in the conference room of the University of Tulsa Athletic Department offices, and Bill, feeling thoroughly contagious but still left out, sat up on the couch, blew his nose so he wouldn't sound too sick, and took part in the draft via speakerphone.[6]

Part of Bill's reason for joining the Galaxy League was the opportunity it gave him to renew great friendships he'd made in college. He laughed often when he was with Wayne, Elven, and other guys he really cared about. Besides hashing out everything that had happened recently and over the years in sports, Bill was interested in their personal lives. Wayne was impressed that Bill shaved and got all dressed up to go to Wayne's wedding, since it was Bill's one day off. I would have been shocked if Bill had not gone.

Bill showed his friendship to others in so many different ways. When Eddie Day, a master control engineer at KOTV, got divorced and was without transportation, Bill stayed long after the 10:00 p.m. newscast, until Eddie finished his duties too, and then he drove Eddie home. Sometimes, just to be there for his friend, Bill stayed awhile at Eddie's apartment and watched Jack Benny re-runs.

Bill not only ate and slept baseball, he wanted to play the game too. At that time, there was no baseball league for guys his age, so he and Eddie helped found a co-ed media softball league. They convinced local radio and television personalities to play on Sunday afternoons, during the heat of the day, since the media people were busy covering multiple sports events on Saturdays. Eddie called it the "Sunday afternoon beer-hall league." [7]

Bill was a great shortstop and fired the ball across the diamond to first base like a strong, talented 18-year-old. One Sunday, while playing against Channel 23, Bill and Eddie turned a triple play. Eddie remembers the great moment in their sports history. "Our centerfielder had brought his

The KOTV Eyewitness News team at Honor Heights Park in Muskogee for the Azalea Parade. It was freezing cold! Left to right, Bob Losure, Clayton Vaughn, Bill, and Jim Giles. *Courtesy KOTV.*

Bill playing softball for the Channel 6 team in May 1982. After Bill and Eddie turned their triple play, teammates pegged Bill as "Triple-play Teegins." When Bill left KOTV, Eddie and their other friends presented Bill with the finest Wilson softball glove. *Courtesy KOTV.*

BELOW: Bill loved sitting in his favorite chair, reading the sports section, and waiting for Amanda to sneak up on him and jump into his lap. He often asked Amanda to play the baseball card game with him, and she did by the hour, long after Janis had grown tired of it.

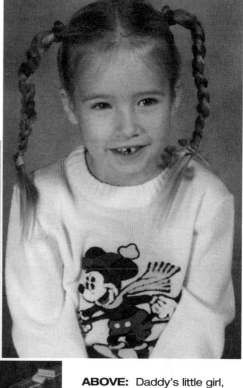

ABOVE: Daddy's little girl, Amanda. On days when Janis worked, Bill helped Amanda get dressed for kindergarten. He could handle a ponytail, but Janis had to tease him because the dog-ears were seldom straight, and Amanda's jeans were as often as not pulled on backwards.

dog to the game, and Bill was concerned that the guy was too busy talking to his dog and would miss a ball that was hit to him," Eddie explained. "With the bases loaded, the hitter clobbered a ball to deep center. Somehow, the centerfielder took his mind off his dog and made a circus catch. I screamed, 'second base.' The centerfielder threw the ball to Bill, who was covering second, and Bill then fired it on to me at first base, to complete the rare triple play."[8]

Steve Mark   Bill Teegins

Bill and weekend sports anchor, Steve Mark, became close friends. *Courtesy KOTV.*

Realizing that even major league players were seldom involved in a triple play, Eddie memorialized the event by buying Bill a triple-play trophy. Bill was thrilled and proud, and of course, I still have that trophy.

In October of 1984, Bill won the Most Popular Sportscaster Award in a poll conducted by the *Tulsa Tribune*. He beat out Jerry Webber, who was still doing sports at Channel 2, and John Walls, who had replaced Bob Carpenter at Channel 8.

The headline in Mel Bracht's "On the air" column in the *Tribune* the next day read, TEEGINS IS HARD TO DISLIKE. Bracht wrote, "Teegins' smooth delivery and easygoing personality appeal to a wide audience." Bill scored in the top two on most ballots. The newspaper printed a selection of comments from polled viewers: Professional and likeable…Refreshing, getting better…Not only a handsome man and my favorite sportscaster, but he is truly a man in every sense of the word…He should get more airtime than those irritating weathermen." Bill and I made lots of great jokes after that.

The question people asked me most about being married to a sportscaster was "What time does Bill go to work, and when does he get home?" Bill's workday started around 1:00 p.m. with an hour or so off for dinner between the 6:00 and 10:00 p.m. newscasts, and his day ended around 11:00 p.m., barring the World Series, or Miss America Pageant that might run the newscast later than usual. We lived in far

When news co-anchor Bob Losure went to CNN, Jill Lyon replaced him. Left to right on the news set are Jim Giles, Clayton Vaughn, Jill Lyon, and Bill. *Courtesy KOTV.*

southeast Tulsa, 30 minutes from the KOTV studio. Still, Bill made it home for dinner almost every night. It was a hard grind, but time together as a family was important to both Bill and me. It was the only lifestyle we knew, and we loved it.

Luckily, my parents lived only a short distance from us and often helped out with Amanda if I was ill or if Bill and I both needed to have an evening out. We spent most weekends with my parents playing spades and eating mom's home cooked meals. Bill especially loved it when she made her famous fried chicken, mashed potatoes, and gravy—topped off with homemade chocolate cream pie. It became Bill's favorite dinner, and he often suggested to my mom that we open a restaurant and call it "Nan's Heavenly Fried Chicken!"

We also enjoyed bowling in a league with Eric and Paddy Sandefur, long time friends of Bill's, who had also been high school sweethearts.

LEFT: Amanda loved playing soccer and Bill attended as many games as he could.

ABOVE: Amanda, left, Bill, and nephew, Bryce Gibson, in 1982.

LEFT: Bill loved being "Uncle Bill" to his nieces and nephews. This is Janis' brother Jim's daughter, Keary Gibson.

Sometimes our two families went on ski trips in Colorado.

After Amanda began first grade, she was gone most of the day, and was usually asleep when Bill came home from work at night. To make up for that, Bill set his alarm early so he could spend time with her every morning before she left for school, often teasing her through breakfast, telling her she'd snow the boys with her knock-out smile, and that she better not replace her "Da" with some freckle faced boyfriend.

Even though Bill's job was demanding and time consuming, he always made it a point to be present at Amanda's activities such as talent shows, school plays, and parent-teacher conferences. We attended church together as a family and Bill liked to read the weekly scripture lessons during the service. I especially loved listening to his voice during those times. He also served on our church advisory committees.

Bill was excited when Amanda took an interest in sports. When she was in the first grade, we signed her up to play on a soccer team. At that age, the coach just hoped that his players ran in the right direction and kicked the ball into the opposing team's goal. Bill had higher expectations than that, and he had no patience. He ran up and down the sideline, yelling, "Kick the ball, kick the soccer ball. For cryin' out loud, *somebody, anybody,* please kick the ball!"

Bill's sideline cheerleading embarrassed and distracted Amanda. Finally, I had a talk with Bill and explained the need for toning it down, and I "banished" him from the sidelines for a few weeks. That seemed to do the trick, and Amanda was able to get her head back into the game.

At home, non-stop, Amanda could con Bill into playing "school." He was always the wiggly, badly behaved student, while Amanda was the dutiful school marm, doling out apt punishments and tough assignments to her ill-mannered pupil. She could also count on him to play Chutes and Ladders and a closet full of other games. Amanda loved Strawberry Shortcake, and she had a collection of miniature figurines that smelled exactly like their names—Blueberry Muffin, Lemon Meringue, and of course Strawberry Shortcake. Amanda had Bill sit on the couch, asked him to close his eyes, and then she'd make him smell the dolls and try to guess their names.[9] I always marveled that he really would do that.

Bill had a special affection for sports heroes of yesterday. In 1985, Bill was asked by Lynne Draper, executive director of the Jim Thorpe Association, to serve on the first selection committee for the Oklahoma Sports Hall of Fame. He joined sportswriters, sportscasters, college sports information directors, former OSU coach Henry Iba, former New York Yankees pitcher Allie Reynolds, and others to compare the careers of great Oklahoma sports stars in order to decide who should receive this honor. Bill spent a lot of time going over statistics and highlights of the dozens of former athletes nominated for induction into the Hall of Fame. He was flattered that he was asked to serve on the committee.

Bill read stories to Amanda while she sat on his lap. Often he was exhausted from his long hours, and would drift off to sleep during a story. "Dad, you already said that!" Amanda would say. "You're not even paying attention! Wake up!"

With all his interests and responsibilities, Bill always found time to show how much he loved Janis and his little Amanda Leigh.

Still, with all his interests and responsibilities, Bill always found time to show me how much he loved me. In 1985, with no particular holiday in mind, just out of the blue, he wrote me this poem which I shall treasure always:

To Janis

I love you very much
My Janis Marie
We've spent each Christmas
Since '73
For over 12 years
You've been my wife
I hope it's that way
The rest of my life
It's hard to put into words
What you mean to me
You and little Amanda Leigh.

Love, Bill

a tribute to BILL

BY BOB LOSURE

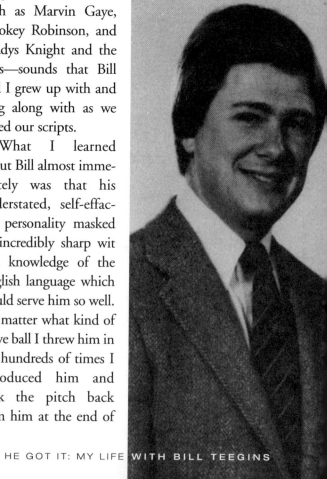

When Bill came to CBS affiliate KOTV in Tulsa from his job in Amarillo, Texas, management put him in with me in a 9 x 18-foot room off the main newsroom. We had typewriters, so the sound of the clack-clack-clack was mixed with the sounds of Bill's radio tuned to stations that played the songs of Motown artists such as Marvin Gaye, Smokey Robinson, and Gladys Knight and the Pips—sounds that Bill and I grew up with and sang along with as we typed our scripts.

What I learned about Bill almost immediately was that his understated, self-effacing personality masked an incredibly sharp wit and knowledge of the English language which would serve him so well. No matter what kind of curve ball I threw him in the hundreds of times I introduced him and took the pitch back from him at the end of the sportscast each night, he was always about 10 steps ahead of me on the comeback. One night he had concluded his time with video of some motorcyclists in a Tulsa event in which they rode inside a 40-foot diameter sphere, just missing each other as centrifugal force combined with the motorcycle's speed to propel them around the cage within inches of each other. Bill ended his sportscast with, "It's amazing those guys don't just get dizzy and fall off their bikes."

I countered, "Bill, somehow I don't see you on one of those bikes." "What are you talking about, Bob?" he shot back, with a mock look of being offended by the remark, "I don't know if you knew this or not, but I did those same stunts in that same sphere just before those guys got on

The KOTV-6 News team. News co-anchors Bob Losure and Clayton Vaughn; Meteorologist Jim Giles; and Sports Director, Bill Teegins. *Courtesy KOTV.*

to ride…and I'm here to tell you it nearly killed me."
Co-anchor, Clayton Vaughn, and weatherman Jim
Giles roared with laughter.

In April of 1982, Clayton, Jim, Bill, and I were
scheduled to ride in the Muskogee Azalea Festival
parade. We did not dream that circling Honor
Heights Park in a convertible would be so tough.
However, it was 30 degrees and the north wind was
howling at 20 miles per hour. We were forced to pretend it was spring and that all the azaleas were in
bloom, while dressed in overcoats and mufflers, hud-
dled together like cavemen trying to keep warm.

As the parade unfolded, we found our rightful
place behind marching bands and floats. KOTV's
Chris Lewis and Mary Ann Massey were sitting in the
cold reviewing stand, hosting a live broadcast of the
parade. As we neared the finish line, Chris jumped
over the reviewing stand rail and ran to our car.
"Quick," he said, "get your car right up behind the
sheriff's horses. The microwave unit failed and we've
been running 'Fat Albert and the Cosby Kids' on the
air. Catch up to the horses and we'll pretend you're at
the end of the parade."

We gunned the car, sped past people who had
completed the parade, and caught up to the horses
who were now laying down a fairly steady carpet of
horse manure as we approached the finish line again.

Then the car died, 20 yards from the reviewing
stand, with cameras focused on us. Bill decided to
dismount the convertible and, with an athletic
move that shamed us all, jumped from the backseat—smack dab into the middle of a fresh horse
patty.

He just stood there, looking down, as the scent
waffled around us. I peered over the edge, then tried
to hide the smile that was creeping onto my face.

Then the car died, 20 yards from the review-ing stand, with cameras focused on us. Bill decid-ed to dismount the convertible and, with an ath-letic move that shamed us all, jumped from the backseat—smack dab into the mid-dle of a fresh horse patty.

"Guys, I don't think we need to get out right HERE," he said. He was not amused, but remained stoic, and still witty, in the face of crisis. Bill said, "Open the glove box, Losure. Let's pray we've got an ice scraper in there." Luckily, we did.

In the world of television broadcasting, it is always a juggling act to make time for your family. For Bill, he was prepared to meet that challenge 24 hours a day, seven days a week. It was no secret that at Sipe's supermarket in 1971, Bill had found THE woman to spend the rest of his life with in Janis, and that their marriage had a rock-solid foundation. In our little cubby-hole at KOTV, I couldn't help but eavesdrop as Bill called Janis several times a day beginning in the late afternoon, finishing their conversations with a heartfelt "I love you."

Bill's little daughter, Amanda, in those KOTV days known lovingly to Bill as "Mandy," was showered with Bill's love. "She's the apple of my eye," he would say, grinning like the proud father he was as he typed his evening sportscast.

"That little girl has me wrapped around her little finger, Bob. There's nothing I wouldn't do for her." And he truly meant it.

> If I have a pet peeve, it's people who talk too much.
>
> **BILL TEEGINS**

chapter 6

OKLAHOMA CITY

*I*n early 1987, Bill was approached by the management of KWTV, Channel 9, in Oklahoma City, to consider replacing sportscaster John Snyder who had announced his intentions to leave the station, partly because of a difference in philosophy with his bosses and his desire to get away from the grind of doing nightly sportscasts.[1]

By this time, Duane Harm, the former president of KOTV, had become president of KWTV. He believed Bill would be perfect for the sports anchor slot in Oklahoma City. He knew Bill's love for sports and how popular he had become in Tulsa. However, there were two challenges. Bill had four years left on his contract at KOTV, and we were happy living in Tulsa.

Bill was interested in the Oklahoma City job because it was in a larger broadcast market—Tulsa was the 52nd largest television market in the nation and Oklahoma City was 34th. Additionally, Oklahoma City was closer to major colleges and universities and their sports programs, and the KWTV job paid more. We talked about the move and I promised to back him 100 percent on whatever he decided.

Bill's original contact with staff at Channel 9 was with Ed Murray, who held the 5:00 p.m. sports anchor slot. Bill had called Ed even before he took the Channel 9 job. Ed told Bill that things were not very smooth at Channel 9. He said, "It is not a rose garden here."[2] Bill weighed Ed's advice, including the idea that, if he switched, he would be working for a while for Snyder, whom he would ultimately replace as sports director. But the idea kept playing with Bill and I could tell there was a strong possibility we'd be packing up.

Bill and Ed had worked together before, broadcasting a championship small college basketball game that featured Bethany Nazarene College, now Southern Nazarene University, in Oklahoma City. The broadcast, a joint venture between KWTV and KOTV, was a disaster from the start. Ed remembers, "When Bill and I sat down, neither the headphones nor the monitors were working." The two veteran sportscasters had to broadcast the game by watching each other's lips to even know when it was their turn to talk.[3]

Bill conferred with KOTV General Manager Phil Keller and News Director Paula Walker, who both recognized that, despite early hurdles, the move would clearly be good for Bill's career. Without penalty, they graciously released him from the final four years of his contract. Paula sent this inter-office memo to the KOTV staff:

> Please join me in congratulating our sports guy, Bill Teegins, for being named the new 6:00 and 10:00 p.m. sports anchor at KWTV-9 in Oklahoma City. Bill presently holds the Number One sports anchor spot in this market, according to our latest research, and I expect he'll reach that same distinction while working in OKC.[4]

When the *Tulsa World* broke the story of Bill leaving KOTV in March of 1987, Bill told the reporter, "It's difficult to leave here, but the challenges and opportunities are there in the bigger market. I suppose it's easier to stay where you are comfortable." Bill said he was

The invitation for Bill's going away party when he left KOTV for KWTV in Oklahoma City. *Courtesy Paula Walker.*

Channel 9 is a huge supporter of the annual Redbud Classic which began in 1983 and grew into a nationally recognized weekend filled with running, walking, bicycling, and wheelchair races. The KWTV participants in 1988 were, left to right, Gary England, Patti Suarez, Kerry Robertson, and Bill. *Courtesy KWTV.*

"not one to hop around" and that he had given the decision a lot of thought. After all, he said, when he'd been in high school at Nathan Hale, his objective in life had been to someday be the sports anchor at KOTV.[5]

Bill and I agreed. Now it was time to swim in a bigger pond.

KWTV had gone on the air in Oklahoma City in December of 1953. It was a CBS affiliate owned by wholesale grocer John T. Griffin and businessman James "Jimmy" Leake. The station's 1,572-foot tower was the tallest man-made structure in the world when it was completed in 1954. *LIFE* Magazine, in an article in its September 20, 1954 issue said the Channel 9 tower was 100 feet taller than the Empire State Building in New York City.[6]

By the time Bill came to KWTV, the station was solely owned by the Griffin family with John T. Griffin's widow, Martha Griffin, at the helm. It was the only locally owned and operated major television station in Oklahoma. Soon, the mantle of leadership at the station passed from Mrs. Griffin to sons, John and David Griffin.

ABOVE: Bill, left, with his sister, Paula, and brother, Scott.

LEFT: Amanda, right, with her best friend, Megan Rice, whose family lived across the street.

RIGHT: Bill and his father, Bill, Sr., in 1990.

KWTV was known for striving for excellence, winning the National Peabody Award and the National Award for Overall Excellence from the Radio and Television News Directors Association. In 1980, Channel 9 had been the first commercial television station in the United States to install and operate Doppler Radar, developed by Gary England, the now standard technology that provides advance warning of severe weather.[7]

A few months after we moved to Edmond, a suburb of Oklahoma City, my dad was diagnosed with lung cancer. I made many trips from Edmond to Tulsa during the next six months until the cancer took him.

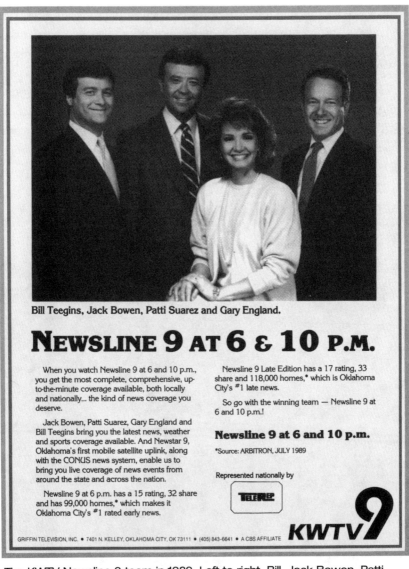

The KWTV Newsline 9 team in 1989. Left to right, Bill, Jack Bowen, Patti Suarez, and Gary England. *Courtesy KWTV.*

After we got over the shock of losing dad at the age of 59, we settled down in Edmond and felt at home almost immediately.

Amanda adjusted well to school and made new friends in Eagle Crest, the wonderful neighborhood in which we lived. She first realized how special her dad was when he was invited to speak to her fourth grade class at

Clegern Elementary School. She remembers, "For the first time, I found out how good my dad was at what he did and how cool his job was and how really proud I was of him."[8]

I was amazed at Bill's versatility and how he never missed a beat. He left his slot at KOTV one day and, practically the next day, began telling his new audience in Oklahoma City about sports as if he had been in their market for years. He seemed totally at ease, until he was informed that he would be required to do his sports standing up, like a weatherman.

In addition to his friendly smile and enthusiasm for reporting the day's scores and sports stories, he also brought to the new position his phenomenal ability to talk baseball, on the air and off. It didn't take long for Bill to meet Randy Cassimus, director of operations at Channel 9. Randy was a statistics comrade who rivaled Bill's incredible ability to recall the most minute details about seemingly the most unimportant players of an era.

Randy was a diehard Atlanta Braves baseball fan who loved to hang out in Bill's office, especially when the Braves game was being televised. Randy and Bill valiantly tried to stump each other with questions about players from 30 years before. While others often grew tired of the mutual barrage and wandered off to coffee breaks, or back to work, leaving the two baseball nuts to themselves, Randy and Bill shot questions to each other like, "Okay, who filled in at shortstop for the Braves in the last half of the 1969 season?"[9]

Within a short time of Bill's arrival at Channel 9, his Minnesota Twins played Randy's Atlanta Braves in the World Series. It was one of the greatest Series of modern times with extra-inning games and numerous tense moments. When Bill came home those nights, he'd be full of stories of how he and Randy sparred as hard in the newsroom as the teams had played on the diamond.[10] I didn't doubt it for a minute.

Standing up to deliver his KWTV sportscast was a totally new experience for Bill. At previous stations, he sat, elbow to elbow with other anchors. But in the late 1980s, it became the trend for a sportscaster to stand up in front of a large green wall on which film clips were shown. The new way might have worked for some sportscasters, but not for Bill. He'd get so involved in the story he was to be reading, he would move with the players. If a football player was taking a big hit, Bill moved his body in the same direction. It was comical to watch.

Bill and Ed were required to memorize their stories instead of using a script, as they had done in the past. That was acceptable if the story was about a well-known major league baseball player or National Football League star. However, if a story was about a high school player about whom neither knew anything, they scattered scraps of paper, story reminders, on the floor. Ed remembers, "We got pretty good at holding our hand out in the direction of the board and looking down like we're just making a move to look at the camera, when we're really cheating and looking down at the floor where our notes were."[11]

Meteorologist Gary England, an icon in the Oklahoma City market, knew the green board idea would never work for Bill. He remembers, "Bill had too much energy. You've never heard so much noise in your life. Snapping his fingers and cracking his knuckles."[12]

Bill was glad when management scrapped the standing idea and went back to the original behind-the-desk format six months later. It made me happier too, with fewer complaints coming from Bill concerning his job.

Within two months of Bill arriving at Channel 9, John Snyder left, and Bill became sports director. He did not mind the additional supervisory responsibilities, but literally hated administrative duties such as preparing the sports department budget and making yearly employee evaluations. When Channel 9 converted to computers, Bill wanted to stick with his old ways, so he hid his electric typewriter in a dusty corner of his office and continued to type his nightly scripts the old fashioned way.

Bill's scripts were unique and to the point. As a lead in to a story about a baseball game, he would write a one line introduction and then type, "Ad lib highlights." He knew the games and players so well that he did not need a stiff, word-for-word description. Bill's ancient technology was king one night when the power to the computer system failed. As the newscasters and weatherman scurried around looking for something to write on, he yelled, over the buzz, "I'm done. I'm fine. I'm good." He enjoyed rubbing in the fact that he was the only anchor who was ready to go on the air.[13]

Television people have long depended upon teleprompters from which they read their stories. But Bill had a special disdain for the machines that often converted his neatly written story or introduction into "xljadoi8usafawjkjf, smclkj." When that happened, Bill read the mistake on the air. No one else could have gotten away with it. Somehow the audience enjoyed him up there having fun. He would say,

"Hey, listen, it says that right here on the script." After he explained what was happening, I'm sure most viewers joined in with Bill's hilarious moment.[14]

Bill was very comfortable on a television studio set and loved playing off any unusual situation, taking it and making it funny for the viewers. He delighted in breaking up his colleagues on the set. His vocal and physical impression of the legendary sportscaster Harry Carey was hysterical. Gary England recalls, "Even though I had seen it 150 times, it was still great."[15]

Outside the studio, Bill was also loose and carefree—or at least that is the way he appeared to his public. Once at the state fairgrounds, he, Kelly Ogle, Gary England, and Jenifer Reynolds were standing near a pig, with at least 100 people gathered around. When the pig walked away, the entire crowd followed. Bill looked at Gary and said, "You know, I've played second fiddle before, but never to a pig." Gary remembers, "It was a beautiful line. After that day, he was constantly after me about that pig. He'd come to work telling me how much he hated that pig."[16]

Bill cared deeply about the quality of his sportscasts. He only had three and half minutes to scan the world of sports and give what he thought most sports fans wanted. Occasionally, he would prepare a formal commentary on a coaching change or controversial topic. After writing the commentary, he'd rehearse it, often to Ed Murray or photojournalist Stan Chase. Bill would ask them, "What do you think? Is it fair? Is it slanted?" Even though Ed and Stan would almost always reassure Bill that the script was fine, he'd go to others in the newsroom and ask them the same questions.[17]

One night, after a particularly hard-hitting commentary, Ed decided to play a trick on Bill. From Ed's desk in the sports office, he saw Bill coming off the set immediately after his sportscast. One of Bill's friends, a reporter from *The Daily Oklahoman*, was on the telephone with photographer Stan Chase. Stan pretended the caller was a viewer who was upset about the commentary. When Ed gave him the signal that Bill was within earshot, Stan yelled, "And if you don't believe what Bill has to say, well just DROP DEAD!" Stan slammed the phone down and used a string of expletives.

Ed and Stan thought Bill was going to pass out. Ed remembers, "Bill was so mad at us. And the look on his face—he turned white as a sheet because he thought we were talking that way to one of his loyal viewers."[18]

Bill was a favorite master or ceremonies for both sports and civic organizations, and he and Janis attended many banquets together.

Bill had a special relationship with photojournalists who accompanied him on stories. Left to right: Dave Tamez, Rick Buchanan, and Bill. *Courtesy KWTV.*

Bill had an unusual way of carrying out his boss-employee relationships with a special knack of turning a negative into a positive. If Ed Murray needed to change something, Bill would mention the change in a matter-of-fact way, then say, "Hey, Ed, let's play Trivial Pursuit." Bill kept a sports Trivial Pursuit game on his desk and lightened up many moments by dipping into the cards to see if someone could ask him a question he could not answer.[19]

In 1988, Bill's second year at Channel 9, he was chosen as the Oklahoma Sportscaster of the Year by the National Sportscasters and Sportswriters Association (NSSA). It was the first of eight Sportscaster of the Year Awards Bill would win.

Bill and news anchor Jenifer Reynolds at the 1990 Redbud Classic. *Courtesy KWTV.*

Bill interviewing fans at an Oklahoma City 89ers minor league baseball game. The photojournalist at right is Greg Blackwood. *Courtesy KWTV.*

LEFT: Bill played in many golf tournaments, including the Pat Jones Golf Day. Left to right, OSU men's basketball coach Eddie Sutton, Southern Mississippi University football coach Jeff Bower, Bill, OSU football coach Pat Jones, and Minnesota Vikings broadcaster Dan Rowe, with whom Bill had worked in Tulsa. *Courtesy Studio II photography.*

BELOW: This group photograph of close friends was taken at Bill's 20th Nathan Hale High School reunion in Tulsa, Oklahoma, 1990. Top row, left to right, Cheryl Mosley, Janis, Debbie Yeakey, Barbara Sandefur, Judy Cameron, Paddy Sandefur, and Nancy Wright. Middle row, Bill, Bill Yeakey, Clif Taylor, Don Cameron, Dale Wright. Front row, Steve Mosley, Jeff Willis, Bob Beasley, and Eric Sandefur.

The year 1990 saw two major additions to Bill's responsibilities. In August, the University of Oklahoma chose Bill to be the sideline announcer for football games. Then, in September, Bill took a page from radio sports with a television call-in show, "It's Your Call." The program aired on Sunday nights at 10:35 p.m. after the NFL scoreboard show.

Bill had wanted to do a call-in show on live television for years and was excited about the possibility of having famous guests to field calls

The Tietgens extended family in 1990. Front row, left to right, Jenna Cole, Whitney Cole, Carol Tietgens, Amanda Tietgens. Middle row, David Cole, Paula Cole, Bill, Sr., and Janis. Standing, Audrey Tietgens, Clifton Tietgens, Scott Tietgens, Kati Tietgens and Bill.

from viewers. The 30-minute program, produced by Bob Lehr, opened with Bill's short introduction followed by a pre-taped biography of the guest. Bill's first guest was former OU football coach Barry Switzer. Weekly calls ranged from 200 to 900, depending on the guest and topic. Later during the Gulf War, OU basketball coach Billy Tubbs was the guest and the show drew 880 calls, even with competing war coverage on other channels.

Of the vast number of calls received, approximately 15 were actually aired during a typical show. Bill told a reporter, "I think the secret of this kind of show is that it is an avenue for the average guy to be involved, voice an opinion, or talk with a sports hero."[20]

One night during the Gulf War, Bill, Rich Lenz, and Ed Murray were discussing the war's effect on the upcoming Super Bowl when they took a call from a viewer. The man on the phone asked the trio if they had ever shot a gun and if Ed and Rich had ever seen Bill naked. Tim Chavez, media writer for *The Daily Oklahoman*, related the story in his "Fine Tuning" column and wrote, "Obviously, there's a National Rifle Association chapter at the Full Moon Nudist Colony."[21]

Bill had an old fashioned push-button telephone for the call-in-show and kept his finger poised over the hang up button in case he had to shut someone off quickly, which came in handy the night the nudist rifleman called.

Bill's overwhelming kindness may have been seen best through the eyes of a 14-year-old fan, Jason Price, of Dover, Oklahoma. When students in Jason's middle school class were given an assignment to "shadow" a business person in a career, most chose a local firefighter, police officer, or city councilman. But Jason was a big fan of Bill and called him at the station, asking if he could follow him around during a workday. Bill was honored and emphatically said, "Sure, why not?"[22]

For an entire day, Jason shadowed Bill and toured Channel 9. The two sports enthusiasts immediately bonded and they met at least once a year after that to go out for burgers and fries. Once, Bill even drove to Dover, treated Jason to lunch, and had his photograph taken with him for inclusion in the local newspaper.

Jason has cerebral palsy, but he sensed that Bill was different than many people who just wanted to help him in order to make themselves feel good. Jason said, "Bill didn't do anything just for the accolades. He sincerely wanted to be my friend and wanted to help me because of our friendship."

Bill was inspired by Jason and often forgot that Jason was operating from a wheelchair because he had so much of what Bill called "get up and go." Bill told me on several occasions that one of the reasons he had such respect for Jason was that he never heard him complain about his condition.

A few years later, during Jason's last two years of college, he wrote for his college newspaper at Northeastern Oklahoma State University. During his summer break, Jason interned for Bill at KWTV. Jason remembers Bill as "very genuine" and one of the kindest people he ever met.[23]

After graduating from college, Jason was having a difficult time finding a job. Bill wrote letters of recommendation in his behalf and encouraged Jason to keep trying and not to give up. A year and a half later, Bill was elated when Jason became the public information officer for the Oklahoma Department of Rehabilitative Services. Later, Bill wrote a letter to nominate Jason for the 2000 Governor's Award for Excellence. Bill said, "Jason is one of the truly inspirational

After Jason Price "shadowed" Bill as part of a class assignment, they became great friends. After college, Jason married Tamara Price and they are the proud parents of a baby son, Nathaniel.

people I have met in my life. He works hard. He is loyal to his friends. He is outgoing. He's an all-around great guy."[24]

In 1990, Bill was asked to give the keynote address at the annual ceremony inducting the latest members of the Oklahoma Sports Hall of

Bill was famous for organizing "Oldies" parties where he spent several days beforehand pulling out old 45's and queing up a fun line-up of music from the 1950s and 1960s. A typical invitation sent to our friends said, "There will be tears on my pillow and pain in my heart if you don't show at the Tietgens pad...A white sport coat and a pink carnation will do, or wear anything that represents those good ole days."

Fame. It was a big night for Bill because he was able to mingle with his heroes. Volney Meece, a veteran columnist for *The Daily Oklahoman*, presided over the special induction of legendary OSU wrestling coach Ed Gallagher.

Indiana University basketball coach Bobby Knight introduced inductee Johnny Bench, the great Cincinnati Reds catcher from Binger, Oklahoma. Bud Sahmaunt, the athletic director at Oklahoma City University presented one of Bill's favorite human beings, the legendary OCU basketball coach and funnyman, Abe Lemons. Finally, University of Arkansas athletic director and ABC football analyst Frank Broyles introduced former OU football coach Barry Switzer. To top off the evening, Bill's good friend, Mick Cornett, also one of his competitors at KOCO-TV, was the master of ceremonies.

For weeks, Bill's conversations were laced with stories about how Abe Lemons told him this or that funny story, how he and Frank Broyles let their coffee get cold talking about sports broadcasting, or how magnificently Chuck Bowman, the Oklahoma Director of the Fellowship of Christian Athletes, gave the invocation.

In 1990, and for the second time in three years, Bill won the Oklahoma Sportscaster of the Year Award. This time, I went along with Bill to attend the NSSA award ceremony. We enjoyed hanging out in Salisbury, North Carolina, with John Rohde of *The Daily Oklahoman* who was voted Oklahoma Sportswriter of the Year.

It was a flattering and heartwarming experience for all of us. Salisbury is a picturesque town located between Charlotte and Winston-Salem, and the NSSA committee members wined and dined us for three days. John said it was the only place on earth where people genuinely like the media.[25]

The morning before the awards banquet, John and Bill played golf at the pristine Salisbury Country Club. John requested he be in the same foursome with Bill, who protested, "You don't want to play with me, I'm horrible." John replied, "Good, you'll fit right in."

Bill shocked his foursome when he parred the first hole, a feat he promised he couldn't repeat. He kept the promise and never made another par. John later wrote, "Therein lies the beauty of golf. It's not about what you shoot; it's about who you play with. Teegins took a bad round and turned it into a great day…for all of us."[26]

That night, ESPN's Chris Berman presented Bill with his award. Bill smiled sheepishly, "more than a tad embarrassed," John remembered. After the ceremony, Bill looked around the roomful of award winners and whispered to John, "Is this great or what? What the heck am I doing here?"

"He was there because he belonged." John later said.[27]

I felt like I had
known Bill forever.

KELLY OGLE

chapter 7

VOICE OF
THE COWBOYS

ill was always quick to point out his "favorite" on any subject. He had a favorite baseball team and favorite players. "The Graduate" and "Field of Dreams" were his favorite movies. His favorite meal was fried chicken, mashed potatoes and gravy, followed with chocolate cream pie. His hero was his father. His favorite band was The Temptations. April was his favorite month because baseball was beginning. The person he would most liked to have met was Abraham Lincoln.

His favorite Oklahoma hangout was Gallagher-Iba Arena. As a sports reporter he often sat courtside reporting on OSU games and wrestling matches. He believed there was something special about the arena that had been named for two OSU sports icons, basketball coach Henry Iba and wrestling coach Ed Gallagher. Both were supreme among their peers. However, Bill never in his wildest dreams thought he could become the voice of the OSU Cowboys.

In February of 1991, *The Daily Oklahoman* broke the story that Bob Barry, Sr., the play-by-play radio voice for OSU basketball and football for the previous 17 years, was leaving to become the voice of OU basketball and football. Barry, sports director at KFOR-TV in Oklahoma City, had broadcast OU games for 13 seasons in the 1960s and 1970s.[1]

Rumors were widespread that OU and the American Network Group, which had acquired the rights to OU football and basketball broadcasts beginning in September of 1991, had already chosen Barry to succeed veteran sportscaster John Brooks who had broadcast OU football games the previous 13 years. Some observers speculated that Brooks would simply swap schools with Barry and become the voice of OSU football and basketball. However, in-the-know sportswriters, such as Bob Hersom at *The*

Daily Oklahoman flatly predicted early in the year that that particular switch would never happen.

Throughout the spring, there was more speculation about who would broadcast OSU games. OSU officials contacted Bill because they recognized his popularity in the Oklahoma City market, which, they correctly reasoned, would be a plus for the Cowboy program in the state's largest radio and television market.

Bill shared his excitement about the possibility of broadcasting OSU sports with Ed Murray. "He wanted the job real bad," Ed remembers, "and he wanted to quickly bone up on radio play-by-play, just in case."[2] Ed found some old play-by-play sheets that OSU's athletic department personnel had generated the previous season. The sheets described every thing that happened in a game, from the coin flip and wind direction, to the individual players involved in each play.

Bill eagerly took the copy, went into the sound booth, and taped a superb play-by-play audition tape. He and Ed later added crowd noise. The next day, Bill mailed the audition tape to OSU.

Meanwhile, *The Daily Oklahoman* kept guessing. In May, sportswriter John Rohde, admitted his frustration by writing in his column, "All you get is a bunch of static. Not even a faint reception…Unofficially, there's no voice of the Sooners, or the Cowboys, or the [University of Tulsa] Golden Hurricane right now—no play-by-play men, no color commentators, no sideline guys."[3]

Rohde went so far as to list the candidates—Bob Barry, Jr.; Bob Barry, Sr.; John Brooks; Tom Dirato; David Garrett; Bill Land; Robbie Robertson; Dan Rowe; Mike Treps; John Walls; Kevin Ward; and Bill Teegins.

Rohde added in his column on May 14," If you're a candidate and I failed to mention you, please forgive me." As the rumor mill continued to churn, Rohde predicted that David Garrett, sports director at KTOK in Oklahoma City, would end up doing the play-by-play for OSU football and that Bill Teegins would be the color commentator. Rohde, like most other experts predicting the future, thought Bill's lack of play-by-play experience would relegate him to a color analyst spot.[4]

By mid-July, Bill had agreed to terms with OSU and its network to do the play-by-play for both basketball and football. Bill was so excited that he could hardly contain himself, but he had to, because OSU wanted to wait until July 22 to make the official announcement.

It was still two months before the football season but both OU and OSU fans were antsy and anxious to know who would be the radio voices of their program. Ironically, both broadcast teams were announced the same day. OSU chose Bill as their new play-by-play announcer; John Walls, sports director at KOTV-6, in Tulsa as color commentator; and Tom Dirato, director of radio and television for the OSU athletic department, as the sideline commentator.[5]

OU officially announced Bob Barry Sr., as their play-by-play broadcaster, with OU sports information director Mike Treps as color commentator and Mark Mathew, the former play-by-play announcer for Iowa State University football, as the sideline commentator.[6]

In announcing OSU's new broadcast team, athletic director Jim Garner said, "In Bill Teegins and John Walls, we have two of the most respected and visible sports personalities in Oklahoma, and Tom Dirato will continue to provide network listeners his incredible insight and knowledge of OSU football and basketball."[7]

Joining Bill, John, and Tom to broadcast the OSU football games were David Garrett, with his "Inside Cowboy Football," a half-hour pre-game

Bill, right, with his famous smile, posing with his OSU color analyst Tom Dirato, left, and Joe Riddle, who produced the OSU radio broadcasts. *Courtesy Oklahoma State University.*

Bill on the golf course with fellow broadcasters, Bob Stevens of ESPN, center, and John Walls, who joined Bill on OSU football broadcasts in 1991.

Bill loved throwing parties, especially the "dress-up" variety. Here Bill is surrounded by Steven Gregory, left, and Clif Agee, our good friends and neighbors.

show. Kevin Ward followed the game with "The Cowboy Network Scoreboard Show."

Broadcasting OSU football and basketball was a dream come true for Bill. In fact, he often said, "Don't ever tell them but I'd really do the games for free." He'd ask me, "Who else do you know who gets paid for having this much fun?" "Only you Bill," I always replied.

The radio broadcasts gave Bill a chance to escape the grind of working in a cramped office and in a studio setting in which he wrote delivered a three-minute sportscast twice each night. No longer confined to the studio, he could sit courtside with the best seat in the house at his beloved Gallagher-Iba Arena and bring basketball action to OSU fans over the airwaves, all the way from Broken Bow to Boise City and Miami to Altus. "That's the greatest thing. To think people are *listening*. They're getting the game through me. That's a real high," Bill often told me.

From his very first broadcast, Bill was a hit with the fans. Tom Dirato said, "From an institutional viewpoint, his image and professionalism provided the kind of person we love at OSU."[8]

Amanda turned 13 in 1991 and was a typical door-slamming teenager. However, that did not prevent Bill from continuing to tell her how proud he was of her, to shout it, if he had to. He often wrote her special notes, always signed, "Love, Da."

Bill learned quickly on the job. For weeks before the first football game, he memorized statistics, traveled to Stillwater to watch the team practice, and spent countless hours with coaches and players. By opening day, Bill knew OSU football from the inside out. Amanda and I knew a good bit of it too, just from discussions around the evening dinner table.

The first football season was a disaster—not for Bill, but for the Cowboys who had no wins, 10 losses and one tie game. It was a totally opposite story in his first season broadcasting Cowboy basketball games— the team won its first 20 games. Bill joked that he joined a school that would never win a football game and never lose a basketball game.[9]

In Bill's second season at the helm of the OSU football broadcasts, Robbie Robertson replaced John Walls as the color analyst. When David Garrett left KTOK to become the voice of the New Orleans Saints, KTOK News Director Bill Simonson hosted the OSU football pre-game show.

OSU fans enthusiastically accepted Bill's excited translation of the events on the gridiron or on the basketball court. They loved his "He shoots, he scores, heeee's fouled." There was always such energy in his voice—he kept fans on the edge of their seats, and often he kept me on the edge of the sofa as I sometimes listened from home. His unique "Teeginisms" such as "For cryin' out loud!" "Touchdown Cowboys!" "Jeeeeez!" "Oh, Brother!" and of course, "He got it!" solidified forever his special relationship with fans listening to games.

Because he was the voice of the Cowboys, Bill was particularly sensitive about treating OSU stories fairly. If there was bad news for OSU fans, he gave it to them straight. Many fans told me, not only at the time, but also in the time since his death, that Bill never took a cheap shot at a player, coach, or fan. Balance, fairness, and honesty were words that fans and university officials used to describe Bill's attempt to balance his close ties to OSU and his job as a sportscaster at a television station a few miles from the other major sports university, OU.

I am forever grateful that Bill was able to broadcast OSU sports, to have his experience of a lifetime. In addition, I am thankful to OSU and

the people of Oklahoma and beyond who shared in the thrill and passion for the game that Bill conveyed as "Voice of the Cowboys." Thanks for listening.

In 1993, Bill helped establish a program to teach young athletes the importance of a proper diet. Covering high school

Before he landed the OSU assignment, Bill probably would have been content to stay at KWTV for another five or six years and then move up to a larger television market. However, the OSU job came at a perfect time— Amanda was a teenager and Bill and Janis wanted to stay put for her.

Bill and OSU basketball coach Eddie Sutton became close friends. Bill could always be counted upon to entertain people around him with a near-perfect imitation of Coach Sutton. *Courtesy Oklahoma State University.*

Bill interviews Dallas Cowboys quarterback Troy Aikman, a native of Henryetta, Oklahoma.

LEFT: Bill and Steve Owens, athletic director at the University of Oklahoma and former Heisman Trophy Award winner.

BELOW: Bill interviews Lee Allan Smith, president of OK Events, about the possibility of a National Hockey League franchise in Oklahoma City in 1992. *Courtesy KWTV.*

RIGHT: Left to right, Bill, Roger Cooper, Jenifer Reynolds, and Gary England made up the 6:00 p.m. and 10:00 p.m. Channel 9 team in 1992. *Courtesy KWTV.*

BELOW: Bill in a 1993 advertisement that appeared in the OSU basketball game program. *Courtesy KWTV.*

THE #1 SOURCE FOR |

IT *IS* EASY!

For Bill Teegins...

...because it's fun!

Bill Teegins, three-time sportscaster of the year, knows basketball like no one else. Join Bill Teegins for all the fun and action of collegiate basketball.

WEEKNIGHTS 6 & 10

SPORTSLINE 9

RIGHT: Bill thought he was in heaven at the 1993 Oklahoma Sports Hall of Fame induction ceremony—he sat at the head table next to the great Mickey Mantle. Left to right, former OU football coach Barry Switzer, Oklahoma City native and New York Yankee star Bobby Murcer, Mantle, and Bill. People later said that Mantle was pleasantly shocked at Bill's great knowledge of baseball.

Bill enjoyed meeting sports personalities at the many banquets he attended. Janis was often lucky enough to attend and meet them too. Here Bill poses with Dr. Gil Morgan, the Oklahoma native golf star. *Courtesy KWTV.*

sports, he saw so many young adults who had health issues, particularly cramps anytime they did a strenuous workout of any kind. He saw how so many of them were out of shape, totally oblivious to modern rules of fitness and nutrition. Bill, KWTV Executive Vice President Jerry Dalrymple, and Operations Manager Dick Dutton contacted St. Anthony Hospital in Oklahoma City to form an alliance to take the fitness and nutrition message to high school athletes.

Oklahoma City Schools Athletic Director Eddie Griffin enthusiastically supported the program, which was called "Bill Teegins' Super Sports." In August, Bill debuted the program at Douglass High School. Bill, two sports injury specialists, Dr. Calvin Johnson and Dr. Randy Morgan, and St. Anthony Score Program strength and conditioning director Pete Martinelli showed an action-packed sports highlight film, followed by a string of sports bloopers, and then stayed to discuss proper eating habits and a recommended conditioning drill. After the program, Bill and the doctors talked with athletes about performance improvement through good nutrition and conditioning. "We really did something good for these kids today," Bill said, after one school presentation, "Today they got information they might not ever get anywhere else and information they will need for a lifetime."

Bill had other interests besides sports. His knack for memorizing dates and trivia was not confined to baseball. He was also a big Abraham Lincoln and Civil War buff. He spent a lot of time in his study, smoking his pipe and reading some of his many books about Lincoln and the war between brothers. He watched the History Channel until the wee-hours, especially if the program focused on the Civil War period.

He loved reruns of "The Andy Griffith Show." I think now, maybe he just liked to laugh. He enjoyed Andy and especially his deputy, Barney Fife. I often walked into Bill's study to find him giggling, *once again*, at Barney's antics in Mayberry. The show reminded Bill of his grandmother Stella Vold's hometown of Lisbon, North Dakota. Bill liked the small

Amanda, left, age 16, appeared in an Anthony's clothing catalog in 1994. She and best friend, Nikki Kaehler, had fun occasionally traveling with Bill on OSU trips, especially the one to Hawaii. To the girl's delight, the "tall" basketball players actually paid attention to the girls and did not seem to mind them giggling and following them around.

town atmosphere, with one stoplight and the safety of not having to lock doors. When he was growing up, he and his nana would watch the three stooges, and laugh and "crack up" together. We even lovingly called Lisbon "Mayberry."

ABOVE: In 1994, The Newsline 9 broadcast team expanded. Left to right, Bill, Gary England, Tammy Payne, Robin Marsh, Jenifer Reynolds, and Kelly Ogle. *Courtesy KWTV.*

UPPER LEFT: As a joke, Bill's sister, Paula, snapped this photograph of Bill, Sr. after he sat next to his son on press row during an OSU basketball broadcast. Bill, Sr. bragged that Bill would not have been able to do the broadcast without him and his "color" contributions. She even signed the photo, "Slick, the Sidekick."

LEFT: Bill, Amanda, and Janis in front of Bill's parents' home in Amarillo, Texas, in 1994.

a tribute to BILL

BY CHRIS HARRISON

I met Bill my sophomore year of college at our annual sports auction. My soccer coach at Oklahoma City University, Brian Harvey, introduced us. I was 19 years old, loved sports, and had decided to change my major to become a sportscaster. Bill sat with me that night for more than 20 minutes, talking about our favorite teams and becoming a sportscaster. Because he was there between the 6 and 10 o'clock shows, he could only stay for about an hour but he spent most of that time talking to a 19-year-old college kid who wanted to get into the business. That's the kind of guy Bill was. At the end of our talk Bill gave me his number and told me to come up to the station and look into an internship.

I interned for Bill at KWTV for more than a year. My first internship was the summer of my sophomore year. At OCU you're only allowed two internships and you're supposed to serve them at two different stations. While I did do a quick internship over at KOCO my junior year, I came back to Bill for my entire senior year, much of that off the books and just between us. By this time he knew I was serious about the business and he was always eager to help me any way he could even if it meant bending a rule or two.

Learning under Bill was the experience of a lifetime. There are two lessons in particular I learned from Bill early on about this business that I keep in the back of my mind today. First and foremost, do things the right way. Professionalism was always high

INSET: Chris Harrison was chosen by Bill as an intern at KWTV. Bill became Chris' mentor and advised him on career choices as Chris moved to network television hosting many popular programs. *Courtesy ABCTelevision.*

on his list. The second lesson, which seems like a contradiction to the first, but it is not, was don't take your self too serious. Anyone who ever had the pleasure of meeting Bill Teegins knows he never took himself too seriously. Bill combined these two simple rules perfectly and that's part of what made him such a great sportscaster.

I graduated from OCU in the spring of 1993. That's when Bill gave me the biggest break of my life. KWTV was starting a Saturday morning newscast. Despite getting hundreds of resume tapes from experienced sportscasters, Bill wanted to hire a young person who would use this job as a starting point to build a career. He gave me the job and that was just the first of many breaks Bill would give me in my professional career. I wasn't making much money doing the Saturday morning show, so Bill let me come in a couple days a week to help around the office even though he didn't need it. He always took time to go over my tapes with me to critique my sportscasts. He was always honest, sometimes too honest, but he was also always encouraging. He even joked about me taking his job some day. His honesty and encouragement meant more to me than he ever knew.

I had only been doing the Saturday morning show for about a year when Bill gave me my next big break. Rich Lenz, the number three guy on the staff, had left and Bill had to fill his spot. I wasn't ready or qualified for the job. Bill went through maybe a thousand tapes looking for the right person to fit in with the staff. After a long search, he decided to take a huge chance and give me the job. Looking back on it now, I realize how ridiculous it was that he gave me that job. But again Bill believed in me. He always did and I guess he knew even then that I wouldn't let him down.

He was always honest, sometimes too honest, but he was also always encouraging. He even joked about me taking his job someday.

The entire sports staff rallied around me and helped me learn the ropes quickly. To think that within a year of graduating college, Bill gave me my first two jobs in the business and I was on the air at a great station in a very good city. That just doesn't happen very often in this business.

By the time I left KWTV in 1999, I was Bill's number two man. It was six and a half of the best years of my life. I have been fortunate enough to have done some pretty neat things in this business. None of it compares to those days sitting in the sports office with Bill and the guys quizzing each other on sports trivia. For the record Bill always won. But in all fairness to us, he always made us ask baseball questions and I have and never will meet anyone who can match Bill's knowledge of baseball.

It was kind of funny but when I sat down with Bill to tell him I was leaving KWTV to take a job in Los Angeles, it was almost like he knew it was coming, he expected it. It was kind of like leaving home for college all over again. I think he knew my time with him was done and he had taught me all he could. He told me he was proud of me and that he knew I would go on to do great things in this business.

After I first moved to Los Angeles, I talked to Bill quite a bit. Whenever I got a new job or a role in a movie, Bill was one of the first people I called. I called him because he got such a kick out of it, and I knew deep down he took personal satisfaction from seeing me succeed. He always cracked a joke about what I was going to be doing, but always followed it up with, "I knew you would make it out there." Bill was my friend, mentor, and even somewhat of a father figure. If someone asks me to name the one person in my professional life that meant the most to me and made the biggest impression, I would without a doubt say Bill Teegins.

I leave you with one of my favorite stories about Bill. He was always taking me on trips I had no business going on. One such trip was opening day of the baseball season at The Ballpark in Arlington. After a few innings we were done with our work until post game. We were walking around the park when Bill told photographer Greg Blackwood and me to promise to not tell anyone what he was about to do. Bill bought three cold beers and took us up to the cheap seats. The three of us sat there on a sunny opening day enjoyed a cold beer and talked baseball. That was Bill Teegins and that was the best beer I've ever had in my life.

a tribute to BILL

BY STEVE BUZZARD

I first met Bill Teegins when he was the sports director at KOTV in Tulsa and I was the sports information director at Northeastern State University in Tahlequah, Oklahoma. He was one of the few television journalists in Tulsa who would give small schools much airtime, but that has nothing to do with how our friendship grew for more than two decades.

In the world of sports, it is rare to encounter someone with such a genuine personality, but I knew from my first professional encounter with him that Bill Teegins was a cut above.

From 1980 until that tragic night in 2001, Bill became as trusted and true a friend as I have ever had. Our friendship transcended the respective hats we had to wear as professionals.

One of the happiest days of my professional life was the day Bill joined the OSU radio broadcast team. He was a novice at radio play-by-play, but he made the transition very smoothly and by the time he did his final broadcast from Boulder, I believe he was as good as anyone in the country.

He endeared himself to Oklahoma State fans because they didn't have to listen long to know if the Cowboys were winning or losing. He didn't even have to give the score, they could tell by his voice if the news was good or bad.

His association with the Cowboys also gave us an opportunity to expand our friendship. It also gave

The KOTV-6 Sports Director, Bill Teegins. *Courtesy KOTV.*

Bill a chance to showcase at an even greater level, his unequaled professionalism.

Bill was one of the few journalists in the country who could do the radio play by play of one team and, the very next day, host the coaches show of that team's most hated rival. He was able to pull it off because it was impossible not to trust Bill Teegins. Whether you were a Sooner or a Cowboy, you liked Bill.

More than two years since his untimely death, I still look at my watch every afternoon at 3:30 and miss that phone call that I would get almost daily and the voice on the other end announcing, "Buzz, this is Bill Teegins."

I would have recognized that voice had he been calling from the moon, but he never ceased to announce himself with both first and last names. I know now that the daily phone call was two-fold. Being the consummate professional, Bill was obviously checking sources at one of the state's major universities. He was also checking on a friend and for that, I will be forever grateful.

Our daily conversations would last anywhere from 5 to 35 minutes and sometimes longer. We would talk sports, predominantly OSU, but we would also talk life and family.

The calls were not one-way. I would often call Bill and try to disguise my voice as a disgruntled sports fan in some make-believe Oklahoma town like "Four Corners." I would rant endlessly about something Bill or one of his staffers had said on the air and he would laugh. These conversations often offered the only light part of long and tense days.

Much of the time Bill and I spent together was on the road and usually around a restaurant's dinner table. Whether we were in Kansas City at a famous local steak house, or in Austin, Texas, or Columbia, Missouri, or any number of spots across the country, Bill's order and reaction were almost always predictable.

Without fail, Bill would peruse the menu, talk about how the last time he ate too much and vow to not do the same. He would then order the biggest prime rib on the menu, eat the entire meal, and walk away from the table moaning about how sick he was going to be. He would disappear toward his room saying, "I'm going to go do my sit-ups and go to bed."

I was fortunate that Bill Teegins was my friend. A lot of people wanted chunks of his time but he was always there for me. I will never forget the numerous mornings I would drive to Oklahoma City and sit with Bill around the backyard pool he loved so much.

I'll never forget Mondays in the fall when Bill would do the 6:00 p.m. sports live from Lewis Field, which meant he spent the entire afternoon in Stillwater. We would go to a local convenience store and just sit for 30 minutes over a soda and talk football and life.

I'll never forget some of the road trips in which we would drive home. One such trip was from Manhattan, Kansas, after the final game of the 1994 football season. The entire trip was one big game of

More than two years since his untimely death, I still look at my watch every afternoon at 3:30 and miss that phone call that I would get almost daily and the voice on the other end announcing, "Buzz, this is Bill Teegins."

baseball trivia. I could never stump Bill in baseball trivia although we had a never-ending argument about the lifetime batting average of Joe Hague, a former Tulsa Oiler and St. Louis Cardinal.

Bill always argued his batting average was higher than I was certain it was. I never told Bill that I looked up Hague's lifetime batting average. Bill was right and I can't wait to tell him.

My last conversation with Bill was early in the week he died. He always wanted to go with the team on basketball road trips, even though it was on a smaller plane. Early that week, it looked like there might not be room on any of the team planes. He had even purchased a commercial ticket to Denver, just in case.

Bill called that week to ask if I could find out if there would be room on the plane. I didn't have the opportunity to ask before he called back to say a spot had opened up on the team plane.

Although a lot of what happened on the night of January 27, 2001, is now blurred, I still vividly remember looking at the list of names of people on that plane before I had to walk to a group of reporters to read them on live radio and television.

That list was made up of 10 men who are precious and who are all missed. The fourth name on that list, however, was my best friend, Bill Teegins.

I can say without hesitation that my life is more complete and my experiences more rich because I was fortunate enough to be able to call Bill Teegins my friend.

Hey, Bill. This is Steve Buzzard. Thanks for being there every time I needed you. Thanks for being my friend. And, by the way, you were right about Joe Hague.

Bill's humor and slant on life made time with him a blessing. The memories and images of January 27, 2001, are still vivid in my mind. I will always consider it an honor to have called Bill my friend and colleague.

OSU COACH , LES MILES

> " If I could retire as a bartender, I could talk sports all day with every customer who walked through the door.
>
> **BILL TEEGINS** "

chapter 8

DREAMING OF A TIKI HUT

F or most of our years together, Bill dreamed of retiring to a "tiki" hut and bartending somewhere in south Florida after his sportscasting career was over. We enjoyed Florida's sun and casual atmosphere, and we both loved to travel.

In 1995, I began working for Delta Airlines as a customer service agent at Will Rogers World Airport in Oklahoma City. Amanda was 16 years old, independent, mature and mobile, and I felt the need for a new adventure. The people I worked with were fun and the flying benefits were great.

Three years later, I applied for a position as a Delta flight attendant, and soon began my six weeks of training in Atlanta, Georgia, for yet another life adventure. My dad had worked as a mechanic for American Airlines in Tulsa for more than 30 years, and he highly discouraged me from becoming a stewardess, as they were called in the 1970s. Flying around in the sky was a job that he thought too dangerous for his only daughter.

But I had my own ideas, and also a very good reason to want the new job. By this time, Amanda was enrolled at St. Cloud State University, near Minneapolis, Minnesota. As I became a flight attendant, I could easily fly to St. Cloud and visit her as often as I wanted. Bill was a great sport, though he teased me a lot about my exotic, and sometimes tropical assignments for Delta. I would call to check in with Bill, and he would say, "Something's wrong with this equation, here you are in Panama City, watching ships pass through the Panama Canal, and I'm doing a story in Mustang, Oklahoma!" Bill was always asking me to check out different "tiki" hut possibilities, and he quickly reassured me that he could take a flash course to learn bartending, and with my great job as a flight attendant, we'd manage fine!

After Bill's death, Ed Murray suggested that a perfect fulfillment of Bill's dream would have been for Bill to open a sports bar in Bricktown, near downtown Oklahoma City, and call it "Bill's Trivia Bar." A great advertising gimmick, Ed suggested, would have been the offer of a free beer to anyone who could have stumped Bill with a baseball trivia question. I doubt that Bill would have lost many beers on the deal.

One of Bill's greatest thrills was in 1992 when Channel 9 decided he should travel around the country to interview sports legends or current stars. One of the early interviews was with Chicago Cubs' announcer Harry Carey, who had become an icon in American sports by broadcasting Cubs games across the nation on WGN-TV in Chicago.

When Bill and photojournalist Greg Blackwood arrived at Wrigley Field for the interview, Carey was running late from a luncheon at a local Rotary Club and was nowhere to be found. Bill and Greg waited around checking their watches, still hoping to squeeze in at least a five-minute interview before the Cubs game with the Los Angeles Dodgers began. The Dodgers were already warming up on the field. Bill, who knew by name, every former ballplayer now coaching for the Dodgers, was excitedly pointing out each one wherever they stood on the sidelines and in the dugout.[1]

Carey dashed in, just in time to take the microphone. He felt so bad about missing the appointment, he invited Bill and Greg to sit in the broadcast booth with him so that Bill could conduct the interview between innings. "Bill acted like a little kid," Greg remembers. "He kept asking me, with this incredulous look on his face, 'Can you believe we're gonna get to sit in the same booth with the legendary Harry Carey?'"

Bill thoroughly enjoyed that game and asking Carey questions during commercial breaks. After a few innings, Carey suddenly turned to the camera and said, "Folks, I want you to meet Bill Teegins, a friend of mine who's a sportscaster in Oklahoma City. I accidentally stood him up for an interview today, and I want to introduce him to you now."[2]

I had no idea that my husband was doing anything more exciting than taking a day trip with Greg Blackwood to Chicago so that Bill could interview his idol, Harry Carey. A few minutes after Carey introduced Bill on the air, John Rohde, Bill's friend and a sports reporter for *The Daily Oklahoman* called me at home and said, "Janis, did you realize that Bill was just on national television, on WGN-TV with Harry Carey?"

When Bill returned home late that night, he lay awake for hours telling me all about his trip. I'm pretty sure that was one of the most memorable experiences Bill ever had in his career. Bill told me all about how Carey required everyone to leave the announcer's booth during the seventh inning stretch, "absolutely no laggers." Carey leaned out his broadcast booth window, and conducted the crowd, off-key in singing "Take Me Out to the Ballgame." Bill laughed when he talked about Carey's face being animated and the famous sportscaster's huge, black, horn-rimmed, "Coke bottle thick" glasses. Bill went into detail about how he planned to use the interview in a piece entitled "A Day in the Life of Harry Carey" for the next month's rating sweeps.

For other special features, Bill also interviewed University of Kansas basketball coach Roy Williams, Los Angeles Dodgers manager Tommy Lasorda, football stars Troy Aikman and Walter Payton, legendary OU football coach Bud Wilkinson, and former OSU football coach Jimmy Johnson. Jimmy told Bill that he was planning to build a restaurant and sports bar in Oklahoma City called "Three Rings." At least momentarily, I'm pretty sure Bill considered applying for the job as bartender so that he could "shoot the breeze" each night with all the greats.

In 1992, Kelly Ogle was promoted from the noon news on KWTV to the 5:00 p.m. slot. With this schedule change, Kelly began spending a lot of time with Bill at the station. From the beginning, they were insepara-ble. Kelly remembers his very first conversation with Bill, because Bill asked about Kelly's father, Jack Ogle, a veteran news anchor on Channel 4 in Oklahoma City. Kelly once told me, "I felt like I had known Bill for-ever, especially when he said, 'I was a big fan of your Dad!'"[3]

Bill's friendship with Kelly grew even closer when Bill and I happened to move into the same neighborhood where Kelly and his wife, Teri, live. Bill and Kelly played golf regularly and Bill often shared with Kelly the rigors of raising a teenage girl and seeing her grow up too quickly.

One of Kelly's fondest memories of Bill is how Bill loved cheap vanil-la crème cookies that he'd buy for less than a dollar a dozen at the local 7-11 store. "Bill could really put away the cookies, especially if Janis was out of town," Kelly says. "He'd eat two rows at a sitting, dunking them in milk until the bottom of the glass was nothing but vanilla crème sludge."[4]

Bill and Kelly spent many hours after work jogging through our neighborhood. Bill would ask Kelly, "Am I the slowest human on earth?" Once, they were taking an evening jog when they encountered an unusual visitor. While tackling a killer hill in the neighborhood, Kelly saw something moving ahead of them near a sewer drain. Upon closer inspection, Kelly realized it was a skunk and gave it a wide berth. He was laughing so hard, he could not yell back to warn Bill, who was as usual, lagging behind. When Bill got within seven or eight feet of the skunk, he suddenly dodged to the middle of the street, shot past Kelly in a flash, and went flying up "widow maker hill."

"He was no longer the slowest man on earth. It was beautiful." Kelly remembers.[5] The skunk incident resulted in a new nickname for Bill—"Skunkboy."

Kelly and Skunkboy spent thousands of hours together in the newsroom and on the set. "Bill was the best sports anchor I ever worked with," Kelly said. "There was never any last-minute shuffling or juggling…no panic. Even if things were going 'kaput' around him, Bill never panicked. On the set, he was in total control, and he knew he could go for two or three minutes even if the teleprompter malfunctioned or none of the video tape machines worked."[6]

Kelly was convinced that Bill's extraordinary ad lib ability and his comical and lighthearted outlook on mistakes during his sports broadcasts actually made Bill's "worst shows" turn out to be some of his "best shows."[7]

Bill remembered with great appreciation the times when older and more experienced broadcasters had shown interest in his career, so he always returned the favor to interns who worked in the newsroom at KWTV. College students loved to intern under Bill for a semester's credit, and Bill was adamant that it be a serious learning process. He insisted they show up on time and dress professionally.

Greg Blackwood observed Bill's tutelage of the interns, "If they showed up in shorts or a shirt that was not presentable, Bill would make them go home." Greg says, "It was real important to Bill to show them that this was a profession and if they were going to get anywhere with it, they needed to be professional."

Bill never talked about anyone behind his or her back—he was casual and right to the point with anything that needed saying, but I don't believe people took offense. "He'd simply confront them with his advice or complaint," Greg remembers.[8]

Co-workers loved Bill. Lisa Liebl worked with Bill for six years. When she began, she admits she did not know a National Football League team from a National Hockey League team. As an associate producer, Lisa was responsible for updating scores for games in progress during a sportscast.

When Bill needed an update on a specific game, he would often request the information from Lisa while running toward the set. "What do their helmets look like?" Lisa would shout back. Bill, still running, probably straightening his tie and smoothing down his hair, would shake his head, and with a boyish smile, shout, "For cryin' out loud, Liebl!"[9]

One day Bill surprised Lisa with a sheet that he had made with a list of teams, their mascot, and a picture of each team's helmet. Lisa really appreciated that kindness. "I never had to ask again," she said, "and I became addicted to football, even choosing the sport over life on Sundays."[10]

Bill seldom allowed interns or station employees to pay for lunch or dinner. After the 6:00 p.m. newscast, it became a tradition that everyone in the newsroom gathered to choose his or her nightly take-out food. After deciding where to get the food, someone had to go pick it up. On several occasions, Lisa remembers that Bill whispered to her, "You fly, I'll buy." As a $6.50 an hour associate producer, it didn't take Lisa long to catch on to the program, although occasionally, Lisa being Lisa, she'd surprise Bill by buying his dinner.[11]

Bill loved his busy workweeks and even if I thought so, he never seemed to think that they were too full. He had more than a fulltime job at KWTV. He also broadcast OSU basketball and football games, hosted weekly coaches' shows for OU's Bob Stoops and Kelvin Sampson, and in some years, hosted Eddie Sutton's weekly show.

Bill often teased that the most difficult part of his day was the 10 minutes he spent live, with colorful, and sometimes outrageous radio personality Al Eschbach on WWLS Radio, the Sports Animal in Oklahoma City. WWLS listeners have told me that they actually anticipated Al's ribbing of Bill about his just getting out of rehab or asking Bill who was next in line to get his job.

Bill also had fun with strangers who thought they recognized him. Someone would say, "Hey aren't you Bill Teegins?" and Bill would reply,

In this photograph, Rick Dalton, left, Tom Dirato, and Bill prepare for a basketball game broadcast at Gallagher-Iba Arena in Stillwater. *Courtesy
Oklahoma State University.*

"No, I guess I just kinda look like him." His voice gave him away every
time, and people would look at him funny, maybe walk a few feet away,
and then come back and say, "You are, too!" Occasionally, someone
would accuse him of being Dean Blevins! He took that as a huge compliment and didn't want to disappoint them, so he'd play along.

Bill was never more at home than when he was broadcasting OSU bas-
ketball games. He was thrilled to be the guy behind the microphone call-
ing the Cowboys' magic carpet ride to the Final Four in Seattle in 1995,
the farewell season of three senior-dominated classes that brought life to
OSU basketball and ushered in the rise of Bryant Reeves to the "Big
Country" legend. Bill followed crucial shots by Darwyn Alexander, Randy
Rutherford, and Desmond Mason with a simple and excited "HE GOT
IT!"

Even with his busy schedule, Bill was always generous with his time to
aid charitable and church-related causes. He served on several committees
and often headed up the blood donor drive at our church, Lord of Life
Lutheran, in Edmond. From his first years in Oklahoma City, Bill gave of

his time to help the Special Olympics. He was a popular guy with these kids because of his warm manner and the fact that many of the participants recognized him from television.

In 1995, Suzi Clowers, president of the Oklahoma Chapter of the Arthritis Foundation, approached Bill looking for a celebrity to host the organization's annual golf tournament to raise money for arthritis research. Wally Johnson, chairman of the golf tournament committee, and Suzi met with Bill to discuss what they envisioned as his role and to formally request his help.[12]

Bill liked the idea of helping raise funds for arthritis research partly because his nana, Stella Vold, has arthritic problems. Bill agreed not only to host the tournament but to also talk about it in advance on Channel 9. For weeks before the tournament, he encouraged golfers to sign up. The publicity was invaluable. Funds raised from the annual tournament increased over a seven-year period, from $20,000 to $75,000 annually.[13]

The tournament was then named the Bill Teegins Arthritis Scramble and Bill was not there in name only. He was very visible around the golf course during the entire tournament. He met and welcomed many of the golfers, passed out awards to, and interviewed many of the sponsors. He broadcast his sports live from the tournament, letting listeners in on all the fun.

"It sure made it easier to sign up corporate sponsors for the next year," Suzi says, "because they knew Bill was going to be there and he just might interview them on television. It was a win-win situation for everyone."[14]

In 1996, Bill also helped the Arthritis Foundation promote a mini-grand prix as a fund-raiser. He convinced Channel 9 to sponsor a mini-racer in the event. In a public service announcement for the race, Bill drove up in his mini-car, sporting his cute little grin and wind blown hair, and said, "Help the Arthritis Foundation put the brakes on arthritis."[15]

That same year, in July, Bill spent his birthday with photojournalist Stan Chase covering the Olympics in Atlanta, Georgia. It became much more than a sports assignment for both men that day because of the bomb that rocked the Olympic Plaza and the lives of many of its participants. The bomb exploded one hour after Bill and Stan had left the Olympic Plaza area to return to their hotel. As the news of the bombing came in,

ABOVE: Bill and his Cowboy broadcast team at Lewis Field in October of 1996. Left to right, Wade Biswell, Tom Dirato, Joe Riddle, Bill, and Greg Blackwood. Biswell was the "stat man," keeping current statistics during the game. *Courtesy Oklahoma State University.*

BELOW: Bill loved to relax at home, on the golf course, or on vacation.

Bill was in constant contact with KWTV and, as he could do so well, became their on-the-scene news reporter.[16]

Because of the Atlanta bombing, a strict security blanket was thrown over the Olympics and the participating athletes. The day after the bombing, Bill and Stan showed up for a previously scheduled interview with Edmond, Oklahoma's Olympian Shannon Miller, who was staying, along with other American gymnasts, in a sorority house on an Atlanta college campus.

As Bill and Stan prepared for the interview, a spokesperson for the United States Olympic gymnastics team burst into the room. "She jumped all over Shannon's coach, Steve

Bill with country music star and Oklahoma native Vince Gill, right, at Vince's celebrity golf tournament in 1995. *Courtesy: OK Events.*

Nunno, for having strangers in the house," Stan recalls. Nunno got right back in her face and said, "Hey, chill out. These are my 'homeys' from Oklahoma City, and they're here to talk to Shannon, not to hurt anybody."[17]

"Well, someone is going to hear about this!" the spokesperson said. Coach Nunno was determined to give Bill the interview and shot back, "Fine, what are you gonna do? Kick Shannon out of the Olympics?" After the lady backed off, Shannon gave Bill an incredible interview.

The New Dimension In Sports

Sportsline 9 let's you become a part of the action...
Bill Teegins, Ed Murray and Rich Henkels for a new dimension in sports...
Oklahoma's best coverage keeps getting better...

sportsline 9

KWTV Channel 9, Oklahoma City

ABOVE: Bill with then Oklahoma Congressman Steve Largent, right, is a member of the National Football League Hall of Fame. Largent was a record-breaking wide receiver for the University of Tulsa in the 1970's and later played professionally for the Seattle Seahawks. In 2002, Largent ran for governor of Oklahoma. *Courtesy: Jim Thorpe Association.*

LEFT: One of Janis' favorite publicity "mugs" of Bill. *Courtesy KWTV.*

BELOW: Bill enjoyed sports banquets because he could talk sports trivia for hours with his friends in the business such as, left to right: Bob Hersom of *The Daily Oklahoman* and KOCO-TV sportscaster Mick Cornett, later an Oklahoma City City Councilman.

SPORTSCASTER
OF THE YEAR

BILL
TEEGINS

WEEKNIGHTS AT 6 & 10   KWTV 9

LEFT: A basketball program that promoted Bill's sportscasts after the first time he was chosen Oklahoma's Sportscaster of the Year. *Courtesy: KWTV.*

RIGHT: University of Oklahoma men's basketball coach Kelvin Sampson and Bill played golf on OU Media Day.

BELOW: Visiting with friends at one of Channel 9's Christmas parties at the Oklahoma City Golf and Country Club, left to right: me, Sue McMillon, Bill, Patti Suarez, and Larry McMillon. *Courtesy: KWTV.*

RIGHT: Our family portrait in 1996, Amanda was a junior in high school. Like Bill and Janis, Amanda loved the Beatles. It was around this time that Bill took her to her socond Paul McCartney concert. The first time, they had to pay so much extra for the tickets because of a sell out, Bill and Amanda left Janis at the mall. A few years later, all three of them went to a McCartney concert in Houston. *Courtesy Taylormade Photography.*

Bill with little sister, Paula, at their parents' home in Amarillo, Texas.

BELOW: Amanda graduated from Edmond Memorial High School in May of 1997. She enrolled at St. Cloud State University in Minnesota because it was one of the few schools in the nation offering a four-year real estate curriculum. Even though Bill was from Minnesota, he argued against her choice, saying, "It's so far away, and it's awfully cold. What about OSU? Stillwater's really great!" Amanda prevailed, as she so often successfully did with her devoted father, and she and her good friend, Nikki Kaehler, both decided to go to St. Cloud. Good-naturedly, Bill drove fourteen hours in a jam-packed U-Haul carting all of Amanda's "stuff."

LEFT: Suzi Clowers, left, and Bill pose with the poster announcing the Bill Teegins Arthritis Scramble. *Courtesy: Oklahoma Chapter, Arthritis Foundation.*

RIGHT: Bill, dwarfed by former OSU and Chicago Bears lineman Paul Blair, who played in Bill's Arthritis Foundation golf tournament in 1996. *Courtesy: Oklahoma Chapter, Arthritis Foundation.*

BELOW: Bill and his best friend, Jon King, on vacation in San Mateo, California, in 1997.

Bill Teegins Arthritis Scramble 1997

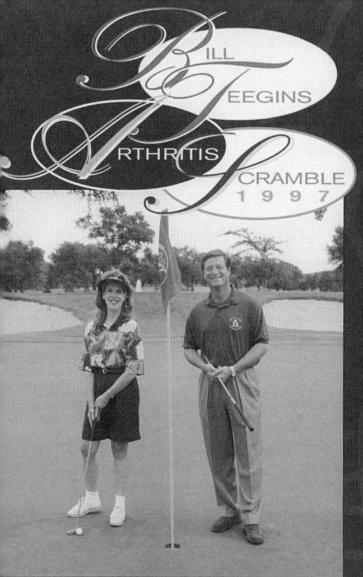

HOLE SPONSOR

Credit Bureau of
Oklahoma City, Inc.
Eberly & Meade
Eskridge Oldsmobile
HEALTHSOUTH
Insurance Resources
Agency of America
KJ103
KPMG Peat Marwick
Mercy Health Center
NationsBank
OG&E Electric Services
Orthopedic &
Reconstructive Center
Osteoporosis Diagnos
Center
Pfizer Pharmaceuticals
RMP Investments
Southwestern Bank
Southwestern Bell
Telephone
Stillwater National Bank
Texaco
UMB Bank
Union Bank

DINNER SPONSOR:
Deaconess Hospital

SHIRT SPONSOR:

MONDAY, SEPTEMBER 8, 1997
OKLAHOMA CITY GOLF AND COUNTRY CLUB

ASSOCIATE SPONSORS:

GOLD SPONSORS:

ABOVE: Bill had a tender spot for Special Olympics. Bill and Greg Kerr, right, add ribbons to this proud Special Olympian.

LEFT: The poster promoting the 1997 Bill Teegins Arthritis Scramble. With Bill is Peggy Henley, a sufferer of rheumatoid arthritis who served on the Arthritis Foundation Associate Board. *Courtesy: Oklahoma Chapter, Arthritis Foundation.*

RIGHT: The dream of a bartending 'tiki' hut life, where Bill could have talked sports all day every day is a perfect example of Bill's love for people and his passion for sports. Janis and Bill never got the retirement dream, but during his working life, Bill already had the perfect job— he lived and breathed sports and was blessed with great friends and family, and a superb natural talent for his earthly assignment. Janis sometimes tells herself, "Bill's somewhere really safe, setting up the "tiki" for me now!"

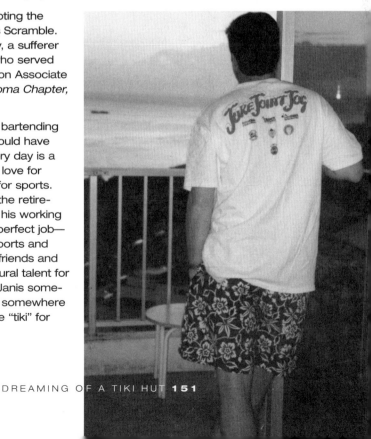

a tribute to BILL

B Y   B O B   S T O O P S

When I learned that Bill, who was at the time the voice of the Oklahoma State radio network, would be hosting my weekly coaches football show, I found it ironic, and quite frankly, a bit strange. I had watched Bill on TV many times and admired his work, but I had serious doubts he could pull off something like this.

Think about it—we play Oklahoma State every year and they are in our same conference. It's not like he'd be calling games for a school we never play.

My reservations didn't last long. I knew immediately that if anyone could do both jobs, it was Bill. He was incredibly professional and I really enjoyed working with him. He was politically correct and had an acute sensitivity to the whole situation. However, what I liked most about Bill was that he was fun to be around. He had such an easy-going, pleasant demeanor. He had a way about him that put you at ease…we always laughed a lot, and he was fun to talk to about things other than football.

The season is a very hectic time for a football coach. There are many demands, but each week, I really looked forward to doing my show and spending an hour with Bill.

a tribute to BILL

BY JOE RIDDLE

I first met Bill at Drillers Stadium in Tulsa in the 1980s at a benefit softball game. He was on Channel 6 and I was at KRMG Radio. Frankly, not too many people knew me, and Bill and I visited only for maybe 15 or 20 seconds. I never realized during that brief encounter that someday he would become my best friend.

Bill moved to Oklahoma City so I had no contact with him until he saw me at an OU Media Day. He walked up to me and said, "Joe Riddle, how are you?" I could not believe he remembered my name. He was just the nicest guy—a genuine guy.

In 1992, I returned to the OSU Radio Network as producer/engineer of basketball and football broadcasts. Bill was already the voice of the Cowboys, so our bonding began. We had so many memorable times. He worked very hard and became an excellent play-by-play announcer.

I remember one long road trip to Alaska in 1995. We landed in a snowstorm in the midst of record snowfall, even for Alaska. At 2:00 in the morning, an earthquake hit and fire engulfed the Captain Cook Hotel where we were staying. Alarms went off and we all had to go downstairs and stand outside in what seemed like a 50-degree below zero wind chill. When we went on the air for OSU's first game in Alaska, Bill said, "Well, we landed in a snowstorm, we've had an earthquake, and our hotel caught on fire. I just want to go home." We all busted out laughing.

Bill and Joe Riddle, who produced the OSU radio broadcasts. *Courtesy Oklahoma State University.*

Bill was still like a kid when he was doing the broadcasts. During Bob Simmons' famous football victory over OU in Norman, I turned to Bill and said, "You know every OSU football fan in the state is calling every other football fan in the state saying, 'Are you listening to this?'" With a gleam in his eye, Bill replied, "You're right, it's not on TV. Anybody who is going to hear this is going to hear it from me!" Bill accepted that responsibility and called a great game.

Bill loved doing the OSU games—he loved the relationships he had with OSU officials and fans. He is the only person who could have ever been the voice of the Cowboys and do the coaches' shows for OU's football and basketball coaches. There was never a conflict of interest and fans of both schools respected Bill.

The only time Bill ever got mad at me was during an OSU basketball game at Gallagher-Iba Arena. One of the Cowboys put up a shot that went around the rim, spinning, bounced off the rim, and then somehow fell through. Bill's call of the shot was really funny—he kept saying "Whoa, whoa, whoa!" When I played the segment back in the post-game show, Bill took off his headphones and said, "I don't appreciate you making me look stupid." I replied, "Bill, I would never, ever do that. I thought it was good radio and you were actually giving the sound of the ball as it spun around the rim." From that point on, I think he always trusted me and my judgment on what I was doing.

We would hoot about things. We did goofy things and stupid things, and laughed. He was one of a kind—a gem of a man that all men should try to emulate.

I never had a truer friend that Bill. I have been through a lot of personal hardships—and Bill was there for me every step of the way. Bill was a great audience for me, because I loved to make him laugh. We would hoot about things. We did goofy things and stupid things, and laughed. He was one of a kind—a gem of a man that all men should try to emulate.

Bill on the sideline during a University of Oklahoma football game at Memorial Stadium in Norman. *Courtesy: Lisa Hall.*

It took us a while to think of how we could really do something different to break through this mold in Oklahoma City of old-time sportscasting.

DAVID GRIFFIN

chapter 9

WINDS OF
CHANGE

*T*he spring and summer of 1997 were difficult for Bill. He kept hearing rumors that the management of KWTV Channel 9 was once again interested in hiring former KOCO-TV Channel 5 sportscaster Dean Blevins. Just two years earlier, Bill had been visibly affected by KWTV's efforts to lure Blevins, former University of Oklahoma quarterback and talented sportscaster, away from Channel 5 to have Blevins replace Bill.

General Manager David Griffin had never kept it a secret from Bill that the Channel 9 senior management team had first offered Bill's current job to Dean. David and Bill's meeting in 1995 still played from time to time in Bill's memory bank. During that meeting, David told Bill, "We're in discussions with Dean Blevins about *your* job."[1]

Since that time, Dean had left KOCO-TV and was working as a sideline reporter on ABC college football broadcasts. Bill and Dean had never worked together before. In fact, they were rivals, both reporting the 6:00 and 10:00 p.m. sports for competing stations for five years. However, Bill had a good attitude about any changes that David and KWTV decided to make. He trusted David's sense of what would be best for the station, and he also believed he would be treated fairly by the Griffin family.

David talked with Bill about hiring Dean, a good-looking, popular, and familiar face to most Oklahoma sports fans. This time David made it clear that if the station did so, it would be for Dean to work *with* Bill— and not to replace him.

"Our recruitment of Dean had been very public, and I did not know how the viewers would look at seeing both major sportscasters sitting side by side," David said. He also admitted that he still wondered if he had

Double Teaming the...

games
plays
players
victories
moments
races
events
highlights
camps
drafts
winners
rounds
athlet-
recor

Dean Bill
Blevins Teegins

TEAM SPORTS

NEWS 9
KWTV
THE SPIRIT OF OKLAHOMA

permanently dam-aged his relation-ship with Bill by offering Bill's job to Dean two years before.[2]

While drafting letters of agree-ment to bring Dean to the station, David recognized the possible conflict he was creat-ing. He remembers, "Here you are bringing in somebody who once want-ed Bill's job, and then actually turned it down. You have two really good sportscasters, two people who love their professions and we're gonna' take the risk of it all blowing up in our faces." Some people looked at David like he was crazy when he related his plans.[3]

In early August of 1997, David announced the change. Dean signed a three-year contract to become a sports analyst for KWTV and to provide commentaries on the 10:00 p.m. Sunday and Tuesday sportscasts. Everyone, either outright or in whispers, wondered how Bill felt about the shift. Bill squelched all speculations when he told *The Daily Oklahoman* reporter Mel Bracht, "There has been a lot of water under the bridge with Dean and me. We were competitors for a long time and now we're on the same team. We've had long talks about that. We think we both under-stand our roles."[4]

To further clear the air, Dean said he had no intention of replacing Bill. "I would not be going over there," he said, "if I wasn't 100 percent convinced Bill Teegins was supportive of me. There's a genuine excitement about working with each other."[5]

Kelly Ogle remembers the time of transition and the stress it put on Bill, "I came to admire Bill on a whole new level during this time," he said, "because a lot of people, myself included, would feel very threatened if they brought another main anchor in and said, 'I want you to sit side by side with this person.'"[6]

"Bill just came to terms with it," Kelly said, "I knew if anybody could make it work, it was Bill. He was just so comfortable in his own skin."[7]

With the addition of Dean to the sports team, Channel 9 also expanded sports coverage in other areas. They expanded the Sunday night sportscast, similar to the "Sports Extra" show that had been successful on Channel 5.

They called the new, longer Sunday night show, "The Final Score," and featured Bill and Dean with highlights of the day's sports activities

and in-depth analysis. The show was immediately popular with sports fans.

Chris Harrison began hosting a half-hour special on Friday nights during football season, called "Friday Night Football," a joint venture with Cox Communications and Multimedia Cablevision in the Oklahoma City metropolitan area. He also had a Tuesday night feature of profiling players, from little leaguers to future hall of famers in "Kids' Sports." [8]

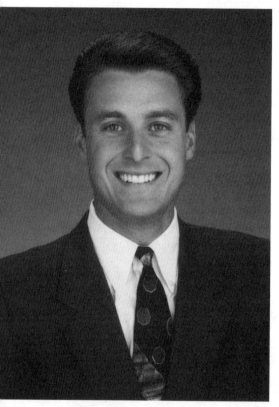

Chris Harrison was on a soccer scholarship at Oklahoma City University when Bill chose him as an intern at KWTV. Bill became Chris' mentor and advised him on career choices as Chris moved to network television to host some of America's most popular programs. *Courtesy ABC Television.*

To make Channel 9's sports reporting even more competitive, David Griffin asked Bill to take a lighter look at sports on Monday Nights with a segment called "The Best and Worst of Sports." On Thursday nights, Ed Murray looked at sports from the sidelines.

Instead of decreasing his workload, and even with an extra voice or two at the station, Bill's duties increased. There were more interviews and added research that was necessary to prepare the special segments. Also, Bill and Dean "chatted" for one hour a week with fans online. Bill fielded questions at the computer from fans trying to stump him with trivia questions or wanting his opinion about some major sports story, or the off-the-field antics of some of the sports stars of the day. Dean answered questions about OU's upcoming football season, new recruits, and the possibility of a change in coaches.

Even though every thing about the Bill-Dean dream team appeared to be perfect on the surface, I knew that Bill was still nervous. Despite his competent, confident, and casual appearance, he also had insecurities. He remembered, and occasionally commented upon, the initial attempt to replace him completely, which had taken place in the not so distant past. He secretly, and only half jokingly, told Lisa Liebl to leave an empty box under his desk "in case I'm booted out and need the box to pack up my things."[9]

A turning point in Bill's relationship with David Griffin came when David invited Bill to ride to Stillwater with him to inform OSU officials that KWTV was in the bidding to produce coaches' shows for OU. "We didn't want to step on any toes at OSU," David said, "but it would be the ultimate for Bill to do the OSU play-by-play and host the OU coaches' shows."[10] The ride to Stillwater broke down the barriers of the employer-employee relationship that had, up to that point, existed between David and Bill. They let their hair down on the trip and became friends from that time on.[11]

Channel 9's marketing department worked overtime to create a series of advertisements to promote the Bill and Dean combination. David said, "They had fun with them. We had fun with them. The ad campaign was brilliant, almost 'Super Bowl-ish' in the quality of the commercials. Viewers liked the promotions and liked the show even better."[12]

David's decision to bring Dean alongside Bill at Channel 9 ultimately proved to be very successful. Bill and Dean became household names. Berry Tramel at *The Daily Oklahoman* reflected, "It seemed a perilous pairing. Instead, it has worked. They are entertaining together, giving Oklahoma City a commentary format and authoritative attitude not found on other shows."[13]

Bill's broadcasts of OSU football and basketball games strengthened his relationship with the thousands of Cowboy fans in and outside the state. By the tone of Bill's voice, a fan, tuning in late, could know how the game was going. Bill had no apology for that fact. He said, "I'm doing games for OSU fans. If you do a game for CBS radio, obviously you do it different."

Tom Dirato, OSU's athletic coordinator for radio and television and Bill's sidekick on the radio broadcasts, said, "Bill's kind of like a fan doing the game. During breaks, I have to remind him, if we get down 10, the game's not over. It brings out the human factor, how much he wants to win."[14]

All is quiet around the table as Bill steps up to the plate. He sizes up the candles-- looks like 45 this year-- and takes a deep breath. Here's the inhale... AND THERE HE BLOWS! Yes, he's cleared the mound of frosting... and the Teegins family goes wild!

Bill and Joe Riddle, the producer of OSU football and basketball radio broadcasts, were both huge fans of Jack Benny. On Bill's 45th birthday, Joe sent this card to Bill. Joe wrote inside, "It's hard to believe you are six years older than Jack Benny." In 1998, Joe sent a letter, purportedly from Benny, to Bill that said, "Bill, I know I missed your birthday this year. I told Mary to remind me but I guess she was busy counting her money." *Courtesy Hallmark Cards, Inc.*

Because of his role as "Voice of the Cowboys," Bill was often identified only with OSU, a stereotype that bothered him. He was still the Number One sportscaster in the biggest market in the state, and he wanted to be identified with all of the schools in the state. This was especially true since Oklahoma is a state where lines are clearly drawn in the sand between the OU and OSU faithful. That fact may be best proved by frequent jokes at parties and the license plates that adorn so many vehicles owned by spouses who attended opposing schools. The plates proclaim "A house divided," with a clear line of separation between symbols of the two schools.

Somehow, Bill managed to survive the crossover. Channel 9 had encouraged him to take the OSU job while, at the same time, they wanted him to host and produce coaches' shows at OU, including the highly popular Kelvin Sampson Show, a weekly visit during basketball season with the OU men's head basketball coach, and later the Bob Stoops Show, when Stoops became head football coach at OU.

The crossover brought lots of comments from fans. David Griffin remembers, "Bill caught a lot of heck. It was rough the first year but many OSU fans respected Bill for being able to do it. That impartiality was what really rang home with Bill."[15]

Most fans thought Bill was fair but, "Some people think you're biased no matter what," David said.[16] Bill's balancing act brought him favor with many OU fans who mentioned him frequently over the next few years as the logical successor to Bob Barry, Sr., who was considering retiring as the voice of OU football and basketball.

Bill truly tried to distinguish between his two jobs. When he was calling an OSU game, he was the school's biggest fan. When he was delivering his nightly sportscast, he was a reporter obligated to present a fair account for all schools. And during OU coaches' shows, he was obviously a big fan of OU sports. Maybe it worked so well because, bottom line, Bill was simply a man who loved the game, loved sports. With all his different assignments, he was a master juggler.

A controversy arose in January of 1998 when the OSU Network crew could not make the trip to Columbia, Missouri, for the OSU-Missouri game because the Columbia airport was closed due to an ice storm. Producer Joe Riddle was already in Columbia and did the pre and post-game shows from the Missouri arena. However, Bill and Tom broadcast the actual game by watching a satellite feed at the Public Information Building on the OSU campus in Stillwater.

Bill interviewing former New York Yankee pitcher Whitey Ford on April 16, 1998, the day that Southwestern Bell dedicated the Mickey Mantle statue at the Bricktown Ballpark in Oklahoma City. Many former Yankees, including Hall of Famer Yogi Berra attended the event. *Courtesy KWTV.*

ABOVE: Bill and his Oklahoma State University football broadcast crew in October of 1998. Left to right, spotter Eddie Nuendorf, Bill, color analyst Tom Dirato, producer Joe Riddle, and photographer Greg Blackwood. *Courtesy Oklahoma State University.*

BELOW: Bill, center, with Kendall Durfey, left, and Greg Blackwood. Durfey produced the OSU football broadcasts. *Courtesy Oklahoma State University.*

The KWTV news, weather, and sports personalities at a promotional shoot near downtown Oklahoma City. Left to right, Gary England, Kelly Ogle, Jenifer Reynolds, Bill, and Dean Blevins. Note the "Why am I standing out in the cold?" look on Bill's face. *Courtesy KWTV.*

Twice during the broadcast, Bill mentioned the fact that he and Tom were not actually at the game. Some fans possibly missed that information and were miffed. Later, admitting that it had been a mistake not to provide more disclaimers during the broadcast, Bill, Tom, and Learfield Communicatons, which owned the rights to the OSU broadcasts, said that that situation would never happen again.[17]

LEFT: The Tietgens vacationing in Honolulu, Hawaii, in 1999. Left to right, Scott Tietgens, Audrey Tietgens, Bill, Janis, Paula Tietgens-Cole, David Cole, Carol Tietgens, and Bill, Sr.

BELOW: Bill with his sister Paula's daughters, Jenna, left, and Whitney, in Lubbock, Texas, in 1998. Bill was in Lubbock to broadcast the OSU basketball game against Texas Tech University.

RIGHT: The 1998 poster for the Bill Teegins Arthritis Scramble. The poster featured a photograph of Arthritis Foundation board members Keli Pirtle-Tarp, left, and Hank Ross. The McBride Clinic and Bone & Joint Hospital in Oklahoma became a major sponsor of the event. *Courtesy Oklahoma Chapter, Arthritis Foundation.*

BELOW: In 1998, Twin Hills Country Club in Oklahoma City celebrated its 75th anniversary. To promote the event, Bill and others golfed in vintage clothing and posed for photographs in front of this vintage car.

Bill was so popular with OSU fans that everyone seemingly forgave him instantly. By then, he was a household name in much of Oklahoma. Paige Keithly and her husband, Kent, were huge OSU fans living in Wichita, Kansas. Paige's grandmother, Alice Smith, would listen to the radio broadcasts at her home in Kremlin, Oklahoma, and call Paige at halftime, and then again at the end of games, with either good or bad news. However, Mrs. Smith was hard of hearing and swore until her death that it was Billy "Deegan" doing the play-by-play.[18]

HEALTHSOUTH. presents
Bill Teegins
Arthritis Scramble

Monday, September 14, 1998
Oklahoma City Golf & Country Club

Hole Sponsors

Bank of Oklahoma
Bank of Nichols Hills
Dobson Communications
Roger Hicks & Associates
Insurance Resources
Agency of America, Inc.
KPMG Peat Marwick
Fred Morgan
OG&E Electric Services
Peak Professional Services
RMP Investments
Signs To Go
Southwestern Bell
Stillwater National Bank

Hospitality Sponsor

THE WESTIN
OKLAHOMA CITY

Gold Sponsors

EREST BROTHERS

Merrill Lynch

cpd
CORRUGATED
PACKAGING & DESIGN

OBBY LOBBY

BancFirst.

BOLDT
BUILDS
OSCAR J. BOLDT
CONSTRUCTION
COMPANY USA

DAILY OKLAHOMAN
SUNDAY OKLAHOMAN

INTEGRIS
Health.

Union Bank
Member, MidCity Financial Corporation

OKLAHOMA CITY RETAILERS ASSOCIATION OF OKLAHOMA CITY

Shirt Sponsor

Bone & Joint Hospital

McBride Clinic, Inc.
Orthopedic & Arthritis Center

NEPHROLOGY CONSULTANTS

Associate Sponsors

KEITH
Ball
PHOTOGRAPHY

OUTBACK

FELLERS
A MARKETING AND ADVERTISING COMPANY

QUANTUM
companies

Bill and Oklahoma Governor Frank Keating at a banquet. Governor Keating sent the photograph to Bill this note, "This photo came across my desk and I thought you might like to have it. Apparently, the guy on the left didn't get the word that it was black tie."

Bill ~ You are very special.

Frank Keating, Governor of Oklahoma

Bill hosted the Bob Stoops Show, the weekly highlight show during the football season. Here Bill poses with Steve Newman, center, Coach Stoops, and the production crew. *Courtesy KWTV and Chuck Porter Photography.*

> An airplane carrying Oklahoma State University basketball players and broadcasting personnel is missing. The fate of those on board is unknown.
>
> **ASSOCIATED PRESS BULLETIN**

chapter 10

TRAGEDY IN COLORADO

B ill began his 11th season as the voice of the OSU basketball Cowboys in the fall of 2000, a real "high" in his broadcasting life. However, for the final two weeks of December, as the University of Oklahoma Sooners prepared to play for the national college football championship in the Orange Bowl, Bill's attention was shifted to Miami, Florida.

Two days after Christmas, Joyce Reed, KWTV's vice president of news and marketing, sent Bill, four other sports personnel, two news reporters, and two technical support staff members to Miami to cover the game. In all, Griffin Communications sent 21 people to Miami, including staff members from KOTV in Tulsa, a station that had recently been purchased by the Griffin family. Two satellite trucks allowed Bill and others to feed live reports back to both stations.

In the land of sunshine, Bill and his fellow reporters and photojournalists descended upon Miami Beach's Fontainebleau Hilton Hotel, the Sooners' headquarters. KWTV called its exciting coverage "The Orange Bowl Blitz."

Bill and Dean began their nightly blitz coverage with "Inside the Game," on the Sunday before the actual play. They attended both OU and Florida State University practices, provided live Internet access for all player and coach press conferences, and asked former OU Coach Barry Switzer to appear with them. The night before the national championship game, Bill and Dean hosted a one-hour Orange Bowl special. The idea was to give the OU fans back home the complete "Miami experience."[1]

Not only did Bill revel in the fact that he was covering a high-profile national college football championship game, Bill and thousands of other

ill talking with University of Oklahoma President David Boren at the Orange Bowl after the Sooners defeated Florida State University and won the 2000 national college football championship. *Courtesy KWTV.*

OU fans were pleased with the outcome—OU won the game and the national championship. Everyone was riding high.

Bill developed a great friendship with Richard Hendricks, the founder of the Oklahoma Sports Museum in Guthrie, Oklahoma. On January 19, 2001, Bill served as master of ceremonies for the museum's Warren Spahn Award presentation at the Masonic Temple in Guthrie. It was another of those precious baseball history moments for Bill. He talked baseball with former Dodger outfielder Don Demeter,

Warren Spahn, the winningest left-handed pitcher in major league history, and Hall of Fame pitcher Ferguson Jenkins. The night stands now as Bill's last public appearance.

Tired from a grueling schedule since Christmas, Bill was still excited as he began the week of January 22 preparing for OSU's road game with the University of Colorado, scheduled for the following Saturday afternoon in Boulder, Colorado. In the Channel 9 newsroom, he announced to Greg

Blackwood that he was going to fly commercial to and from Colorado because color analyst Tom Dirato was riding with Coach Eddie Sutton on one of the private airplanes that OSU often used to transport team members, athletic department personnel, and game broadcasters. This had been the plan, but I knew that Bill was upset because flying commercial would have meant that he would probably miss co-worker, Randy Cassimus,' 40th birthday party also scheduled for later that Saturday evening.[2]

On Saturday, January 27, OSU played a 2:00 p.m. MST game in the Coors Events Center in Boulder. Thirty minutes before the game, Bill used his cell phone to return Amanda's call of earlier in the day. She'd seen on television that the weather was bad in Colorado and left her dad a cell message, asking him to be careful. When he reached her, she warned again, "You know how I worry when you fly on those tiny planes." Bill assured her that he would be careful. Amanda remembers that he even

Bill as master of ceremonies at the Warren Spahn Award Banquet. Left to right, Hall of Fame pitcher Warren Spahn, Bill, and Arizona Diamondbacks pitcher Randy Johnson, recipient of the award.

laughed, probably finding it endearing this his young daughter was shifting the roles and cautioning him.

"Amanda, I'll be okay," he told her. As it turns out, those were his last words to the child that he so loved. [3]

Bill called the game, which OSU lost, and then accompanied the team to the Jefferson County Airport. While I still thought Bill was taking a commercial flight, plans for his return to Oklahoma had been changed sometime during the hectic week, and he was assigned to one of the three planes OSU had chartered for the day.

Shortly after 6:00 p.m., Bill and nine others boarded a Beechcraft Super King Air 200, a twin-engine turboprop. A winter storm was moving through the area, so veteran pilot Denver Mills and co-pilot Bjorn Fahlstrom wanted to get on their way. They taxied directly from a warm hangar onto the runway on which light snow was already beginning to fall. At the time, an icing advisory warned of a "light to moderate threat."

Federal Aviation Administration (FAA) records show that the plane took off at 6:19 p.m. CST. The crew took the aircraft to 23,000 feet and successfully cruised for three minutes before air traffic controllers suddenly lost all contact with the pilots—only 18 minutes into the flight. There was never a distress call. Never a word of warning. [4]

Following standard aviation procedures, within the minute that contact was lost, the FAA notified law enforcement authorities that a plane was missing in the area approximately 40 miles west of Denver. At about the same time that the FAA alerted authorities that the plane was missing, the two other airplanes carrying OSU personnel left the Jefferson County airport for Stillwater, heading into the same icy skies.

Over the next few hours—while I served juice and cocktails to passengers on an airplane a thousand miles away, while Amanda and her boyfriend, Tony, watched television at a friend's house, and while Bill's parents shared a bowl of popcorn and turned on the evening news, the whole world began to understand what can happen to a small plane on a socked-in winter night.

Bill's plane plunged into a deserted snow and ice-covered field near the town of Byers, Colorado, leaving debris, the newspaper later reported, for nearly a mile. The FAA pinpointed the time of crash at 6:38 p.m. CST. Larry Pearson, a farmer who lived near the site, was the first person on the

The last Tietgens family photograph
taken at St. Cloud, Minnesota, in the fall of 2000.

scene and described how the plane's engines sputtered and the aircraft appeared to attempt to climb before crashing in a fireball.[5]

Later, the National Transportation Safety Board (NTSB) released its official report, which said that the plane lost electrical power and began to plummet toward the ground. In twilight and cloudy conditions, the plane reached speeds of 350 miles per hour as the dive deepened. At one point, the report said, the plane spiraled downward at a rate of 15,000 feet per minute, a condition pilots call "graveyard spiral". In just over 90 seconds, the plane went from a safe, homeward bound leveling off at 23,000 feet to impact.

The NTSB later concluded that the pilot had not appropriately managed the workload associated with troubleshooting the electrical failure to maintain positive control of the aircraft.[6]

There were no survivors among the 10 men on Bill's airplane. Killed along with Bill were radio engineer Kendall Durfey, basketball operations director Pat Noyes, athletic trainer Bryan Luinstra, assistant director of athletic media relations Will Hancock, student and educational television services employee Jared Weiberg, basketball players Dan Lawson, Jr., and Nate Fleming, and pilots Denver Mills and Bjorn Fahlstrom.[7]

However, I was not aware of anything that was happening. As I left my Delta flight that evening in Boston, Massachusetts, and headed for the apartment flight attendants shared, I wondered in passing, but certainly not with any sense of alarm, why I had not yet heard from Bill. When either of us was on the road, we frequently called each other, with simple things such as, "How was your day? Were we eating home or out that night? Had Bill remembered to phone Jon back about some weekend plan?"

As I entered my apartment near Logan Airport, after being in the air for the past nine hours, I had two things on my mind—kicking off my shoes and hearing Bill's voice.

Meanwhile, Oklahomans were already learning about the tragedy. Within an hour of the crash, the Associated Press, ESPN television, CNN, and television stations all over the state reported that one of the planes carrying the OSU basketball team was overdue. At 8:30 p.m., the two other planes landed safely in Stillwater, but to a rather subdued crowd of fans. The night was freezing and windy, the game had not been a winner, and, where, people were beginning to ask, was the third plane?

Tom Dirato, color analyst for the games, rode on one of the safe planes, having been reassigned from the doomed plane to one of the faster, larger planes because he had been suffering from back problems all week long.[8]

The news of the missing plane shocked and began to fray the nerves of personnel on duty in the KWTV newsroom. Greg Blackwood was already at Randy Cassimus' birthday party when he heard the first worried whispers. Immediately—hoping strongly that Bill had taken the commercial flight he'd mentioned earlier that week—Greg rushed to the television station and searched Bill's desk for his itinerary. As he rummaged through papers in Bill's work area, and found no itinerary, his fear indicators mushroomed.[9]

Joyce Reed found Greg in Bill's office digging frantically for some bright thread, some small proof that, even if something was wrong with the third plane, his friend was not on it, his friend was still alive. With tears streaming, Joyce delivered the bad news. "I talked to Coach Sutton," she told Greg softly. "There was a third plane and Bill's on it."[10]

At 10:30 p.m., Amanda, at a friend's house, in St. Cloud, was thinking about going home to get some rest. She learned about the missing plane when Nikki Kaehler, her long time friend and roommate, reached her by phone. Amanda turned on CNN, heard the report, and immediately called KWTV. Greg, whom Amanda knew, answered but could not bring himself to tell his friend's little girl the grim news. "Nothing is for sure right now," he told Amanda. "The last thing your Dad told me was that he was mad because he had to fly commercial, so I'm looking for his itinerary right now. At 11:30 p.m., I still think he's gonna pull into Will Rogers World Airport."[11]

Amanda was hysterical, bawling, and throwing up. Somehow she knew Greg was not telling her the truth. Over and over, she had said to him, "You're lying, You're lying!" In the end, Greg said only, "Amanda, you need to call your mother."[12]

My first news came in a frantic phone call from Nikki. I had kicked off one shoe and pulled my key from the apartment door when the cell phone in my purse rang. I answered softly because I was pretty sure that my landlady, United Airlines flight attendant, Elaine Lawrence, was sleeping, trying to recover from jet lag after her usual international flight.

"Janis, an OSU plane is missing," Nikki began. I had never heard such panic and concern in Nikki's voice. "It's all over the news. Two planes made it back from Colorado—one didn't," she ran on. "Have you heard from Bill? I'm trying to reach Amanda."

I assured Nikki that I would try to find out something.

My heart began to pound fast and hard as I picked up Nikki's panic. It ran through my mind with some sort of sick certainty that *this* was why I had not talked to Bill, *this* was why I had not been able to contact him. Was this why he hadn't called me? Was he, and his sporty new black and orange cell phone, somewhere in a plane that had crashed?

And he worried about me—my dangerous job as a flight attendant. He teased me, always, and said that I should get a safe job like his, as a sportscaster.

Before I could even gather my thoughts, my cell phone rang again. "Mom," Amanda screamed, "Is it true? Is my Dad dead?"

"Oh no," I thought, "Nikki has reached Amanda before I could."

"Amanda, don't jump to conclusions," I said, "Wait until I find out if he was even on that plane. I'll call you right back, as soon as I know something."

Adrenalin raced through my body, while my mind scrambled for an explanation—any explanation. I remembered seeing a United Airlines ticket lying on the dining room table. Maybe he took the commercial flight since the weather was not good. Maybe he had gotten sick. *God, let him have gotten sick!* Maybe he stayed over.

I tried to remember the telephone number to the Channel 9 news desk but I was shaking so hard I could not push the small squares with the numbers on my cell phone. I dialed the wrong number several times. I remembered the direct number to Bill's desk, but no one would be there to answer that line. My next thought was to dial long distance information, hoping that they would have the number to Channel 9's Oklahoma City news desk, or any number for that matter that would link me to somebody, anybody, at Bill's work. The last four numbers of Channel 9's staff telephone numbers were all similar so, with my hands quivering, I began punching in numbers. Thankfully, on about the fourth try, it worked.

"News Nine assignment desk," a woman answered.

All I said was my name.

There was a long pause, then, softly the woman said, "Kelly, you'd better take this—it's Janis."

I knew from the sound of this anonymous woman's voice—even though I could not admit it to myself—that the news was not good. I think a part of me knew. The third plane had crashed and Bill had died.

After a moment of silence, our neighbor and friend, Kelly Ogle, picked up the phone and said, "Janis, Bill's dead. I am so, so sorry." Kelly later apologized for his frankness. He said, "I wish I would have said, 'We lost him' or 'He's gone.'" But then, it was not like something you get to practice ahead of time.[13]

Kelly had learned of the tragedy while he and his wife, Teri, watched a rented movie at home. Joyce Reed called him from the newsroom. She was crying and said, "The plane is missing and they think Bill is on it."[14]

As Kelly told me what he knew, my legs buckled underneath me and I fell to the cold, shag-covered apartment floor. My world had collapsed in one thunderous instant. My heart and body ached and I blurted out something stupid like, "I'm too young to be a widow." I screamed, "Bill's too young to die. No, it can't be true. God, don't let this be true."

The stillness of my empty Boston room brought me back to reality. My mind raced with questions. How will I tell Amanda? How will I tell Bill's parents? How will I tell his best friend, Jon King, and so many people who love him?

"Janis, can I call someone for you?" Kelly asked tenderly, and I realized that he was still on the line.

I was crying uncontrollably, but I managed to say, "Yes, please call Bill's parents." I could not handle the thought of delivering the bad news to Bill's mother and father—I needed all my energy to tell our daughter Amanda.

I could not stop shivering. My mind bounced from frantic thought to frantic thought. Had Bill known? Had he gotten settled and—hopefully, gratefully—immediately fallen asleep in his cramped seat? Had he tried to call me before takeoff? Was he telling some crummy sports story and not even aware? Was it pure chaos? Was luggage flying everywhere? Did he cry out? I was horrified to think about what Bill had gone through a few hours earlier. I kept stepping outside myself, putting it out of my head, telling myself to calm down and breathe.

Here I was in Boston, reaping the benefits of a mid-life career. Amanda was footloose and fancy free at college. And Bill was laying in a lonely field somewhere in Colorado. How could I pick up the phone and tell our little girl, "Yes honey, while neither one of us was looking, your Da died?"

From the moment she was born, with her red hair and dimpled cheeks, just like her Dad's, Bill loved this child more than his own life. Their close relationship was far greater than just a normal father-daughter relationship—she was our only child. Sitting on that drab, dated Boston carpet, I kept trying to see the numbers to dial her but kept seeing instead baby Amanda toddle up to the television screen and slobber baby kisses on her Da's face.

Suddenly, I realized that I was as cold as if I stood in the snowy field where Bill lay. I wrapped myself in an old blanket and for a few spacey moments let the scenes come. Amanda turning nine. What a fan of Paul McCartney! McCartney's band making a rare appearance in Dallas and the concert all sold out. Bill paying a scalper several hundred dollars for two tickets and the two of them hopping into the car with peanut butter sandwiches, coffee, and Amanda's homemade poster, "We Love You, Paul." I kept staring at a vase of gaudy red and blue silk hotelish flowers that I'd never liked. Some how that night, I loved them—they reminded me of the Hawaiian shirt that Bill wore to his last father-daughter dance with this child I would, in one more minute, have to call.

It was an oldies party. They dressed up. Amanda wore a gray felt skirt, with a pink poodle embroidered on the front, her hair in a high ponytail. Bill bought his red, blue, and yellow flowered shirt to wear with his crisp, new blue jeans, just to please her. He'd slipped a pink carnation bracelet over her wrist. I pinned a matching carnation on his lapel. She teased him about it, but grinned with such pride.

Then the phone rang again. It was Amanda. I had to confirm the fact that our greatest fears were true.

"Amanda, your dad is dead. Sweetheart, I am so sorry," were the words she remembers me saying, although all I remember is trying to choke back my grief, to be the *grownup*, but could not. All those miles apart, we just sat, each gripping our stupid cell phones, and sobbed.

"I knew it was true," she said with despair in her young voice, "How could God let this happen?" "He's my dad. What are we going to do without him? How can we live without him?"

I tried to console and reassure her that we *would* live without him, though I too had no idea how. We would—unfortunately, I remember thinking—go on without him. But, then again, being "mom," I think I said something like, "Amanda, you know Daddy's strong faith. He's with God this second. It was an accident, a horrific tragedy." Engulfed with the need to hold my baby, I blurted out, "I wish I could wrap my arms around you, baby, and comfort you."

"Mom, you've got to come home!" she said, sounding nine years old again.

It was 11:00 p.m. Eastern time, and there were no flights available to Oklahoma City at that hour. I told Amanda that I needed her too and would make arrangements to meet her in Atlanta, Georgia, the following morning—we would fly the final leg home together. At least, she was with friends at college. I later learned that they sat with her all night, listening to her as she tried to figure out what on this crazy earth had happened— and what to do next.

Waves of memories faded on and off with the reality of the horrible realization that Bill was gone. He had been snatched from our lives. Surely, this could not be happening.

The entire first night was insane for me. I could not stop trembling. My mind went from a single thought to a hundred thoughts. I wrote Bill's obituary on a stack of Christmas napkins, hoping that if I wrote it over and over, maybe it would not be true. I filled the scraps of paper with funeral plans. There were so many questions. Who would speak? Who would sing? Who would be pallbearers? "How do I make plans like this for the love of my life?" I kept asking out loud.

I lost track of time in that dull, empty, rented bedroom, a room that suddenly felt too far away from everything on earth that mattered to me. I tried to muffle my sobs and wails of despair, but Elaine woke up and stumbled upstairs to check on me. I had only been renting a room from her for a few months and I felt weird telling a near stranger something so personal and devastating. Even though Elaine had taken a sleeping pill a few hours earlier and was still groggy, she too was shaken badly. We cried together for what surely was hours.

"Janis, what can I do for you?" she pleaded, the first of many to voice such an earnest, human desire. Unfortunately, no one could do anything. I was thankful I was not in some empty hotel room though, without any-one to reason with me and help me through the start of this madness. Elaine did brew tea, and she offered me cookies, that I could not look at, let alone eat. In addition, she offered to call a taxi to take me to the air-port when I was ready to go.

Surely, I would not need a taxi in the morning, I thought. How would I even last the night?

Hearing that Bill was dead left me with a feeling of being kicked in the gut with the sharpest toed boots possible.

ELVEN LINDBLAD

chapter 11

THE
AFTER SHOCK

*T*he people at KWTV, unfortunately, had two roles to fill the night of the crash. They were heartbroken because their friend was dead—but their professional responsibility was to go on the air quickly, and often, and appropriately tell the story over and over again to their viewers.

Alex Cameron was the weekend news anchor and had left the station after the 6:00 p.m. newscast to attend an engagement party for two Channel 9 staffers. When he heard about the missing OSU plane, between raising a toast to his two co-workers, and answering cell phone calls from Channel 9, he and his wife, Ann, rushed back to the station.

Sometime after 9:30 p.m., when the news was rolling in about the ill-fated flight, and the possibility that Bill Teegins may have been on board, Alex and co-anchor Amy Hawley decided to begin the 10:00 p.m. newscast early. Most of the information they had so far relayed to viewers was coming from the Associated Press. The producer decided to forego commercials and stay live with anything new that came in. For the first half hour, Alex and Amy had a glimmer of hope because no concrete details had been released by authorities.[1]

Jenifer Reynolds, a more experienced newscaster, replaced Amy on the set. It was almost impossible, for Alex and Jenifer, who had worked closely with Bill for more than 10 years, to talk about the story without tears. Alex remembers, "It was surreal because on some level we were sitting there doing our job. Most days, we talk about somebody dying, a plane crash or car wreck, and don't think too much about it. But this was different—we were going through the same motions but we were talking about someone we all knew and loved very much."[2]

Soon, Kelly Ogle rushed in, cutting short his leisure time at home with his family, and without his necktie, and replaced Alex on the set. Kelly, who considered Bill his best friend at the station, and Jenifer, who had such a special relationship with Bill, were obviously grief-stricken as they tried to relate the latest details. When it was all grimly known and the names of those killed were read by OSU officials in a live news conference in Stillwater, Kelly and Jenifer had to take a few moments to compose themselves.

"It was unbearable," Alex remembers. When Jennifer could stop crying, she said in a broken voice, "Our hearts are just breaking right now…I think we knew we were gonna' hear this name, but it's still so very hard to hear it."[3]

At home, senior Channel 9 photojournalist Bill Merickel, who shared a Minnesota heritage with Bill, watched the coverage, especially when OSU Sports Information Director Steve Buzzard read the names of the people lost in the crash. "I kept saying, 'Please don't say 'Bill,'" he remembers. When the OSU spokesperson read Bill's name, Bill Merickel was devastated.[4]

The newsroom was still functioning, but staffers operated on automatic pilot. Kelly's pastor, Reverend Craig Etheredge, arrived at the station, without having to be called, to give comfort to the people who still had a job to do. Someone asked Alex to write Bill's obituary and he began looking at old videotape to use in a tribute. Alex also immediately volunteered to fly to Colorado so that he could report the story from the scene of the crash, and from that point forward, the OSU tragedy became Alex's assignment.[5]

KWTV opened its full switchboard to handle the large volume of calls from well-wishers. Terry Alexander, David Griffin's administrative assistant, and others donned earphones and manned the switchboard until after 3:00 a.m. Calls came in flurries, the first call came from Florida—a fan, who knew Bill's name, happened to hear the story on ESPN. The calls were from at least a dozen states and from every section of Bill's adopted state of Oklahoma.[6]

Just before midnight, an older lady pulled up in front of the station and brought a bouquet of flowers to the door. She started crying and said Wal-Mart was the only place she could purchase flowers at that late hour.

A few minutes later, a young couple brought a sympathy card. "After the three of us hugged and cried together for a while, they just walked away, holding each other." Terry Alexander remembers.7

One man arrived at the station and then, seemingly, didn't know why he was there. He said he just wanted to be with others who were having the same feelings. He paced around the lobby until he thought he might be in the way, and then quietly slipped out the door and went home.

A large basket was placed on Channel 9's reception desk for the hundreds of cards that Oklahomans began dropping off at the station over the next few days. "For weeks the station was like a tomb," Terry says, "except for the sobbing heard in the hallways and in the offices. Everyone was so emotionally drained."8

Miles away, and early the next morning, I took a taxi to Boston's Logan Airport. I knew I would not be able to explain my situation to the gate agent, so I wrote a note ahead of time saying that my husband had been killed the night before in the OSU plane crash. I asked for two things—privacy and help with my luggage.

Because I was a fellow employee of Delta Airlines, the gate agents went out of their way to help me in any way they could. An agent I'd never seen before walked on board with me, lifted my bag to an overhead bin, and seated me in an empty row in first class. I watched as she showed my note to the lead flight attendant—they both looked my way, shocked and concerned.

The entire crew was so kind, and I've wondered since if I even thanked them. Occasionally, they brought me tissues. One flight attendant sat in the empty seat next to me for a while, held my hand, and we quietly cried together.

The night before the accident, I was on my last flight for the day, strapped in my jump seat, with only a couple of seconds before landing at Washington's National Airport, when suddenly the Captain pulled our airplane up and in a steep right turn, and aborted our landing. After we leveled out, the Captain announced that he and the co-pilot had spotted a small plane sitting on the runway where we were scheduled to land. I couldn't help recanting the near miss I had experienced less than 24 hours before Bill's death. I kept wondering if it was God's way of preparing me by giving me strength that I would need in the coming days. Then, after Nikki's call and all the ones that followed, I had not slept. I was exhausted, but still miles from sleep, so I buried my head in a wad of pillows and stared out the window or wept. The two and a half hour flight from Boston to Atlanta seemed like an eternity. I had no idea what I would say to Amanda—what I could say to Amanda? My mind was cluttered with the unfinished arrangements that I would be expected to make when I arrived home in Oklahoma City.

In shock and disbelief, I kept planning things like a crazed robot. Somewhere below the surface, I think I felt that I could still make this nightmare right, if I could just do all the right things fast enough. But everything seemed to be moving in such slow motion. I kept thinking, "Everything is up to me! I am supposed to do something!" But, what was everything? In the end, all I could do was cry, and hope that I would not disturb the other passengers. I couldn't force myself to eat, but my flight attendant training stuck with me—I drank water and juice to avoid dehydration.

At Atlanta's Hartzfield Airport, I trudged along the crowded corridor, noticing the families walking hand in hand, my heart hurting and wanting to be able to do the same with Bill and Amanda. At the magazine stand, I couldn't bear to see if the headlines yet blurted out my new life.

When I found the gate where Amanda would arrive from Minnesota, I stood against the wall and scanned the faces of every person walking from the jet way. Finally, I spotted hers, sweet, as always, and stained with tears. Amanda's boyfriend, Tony Ascheman, was with her. All three of us hugged and sobbed, not caring what other people might think. Those embraces must have lasted five minutes.

It was maddening waiting at the gate for our connecting flight to Oklahoma City. CNN kept running a story about the crash. The reporter read Bill's name, once even mispronouncing it, and there for the world to see, and for us to have to sit and watch over and over, they showed the plane's wreckage strewn for hundreds of yards all about the icy field.

The Oklahoma-bound passengers talked about how Oklahoma had suffered yet another tragedy. Sometimes they listed them. There was the Murrah Building bombing, the 1999 tornado—now this. One woman said, "I can't believe Bill Teegins was on that plane. We'll never see him do our sports again." Her husband agreed, "Well, that's that. He'll never call another OSU game," and as he tossed his empty coffee cup into the trash receptacle, and added, "Bill was so professional and seemed like such a nice guy."

I wanted to speak up and say, "He was. He was a really nice guy!" But I couldn't talk and I couldn't stand there another moment not talking, so I walked to another section of the airport where people enroute to other states just thumbed through magazines or talked about the weather or what they'd done that weekend.

Closer to departure time, I returned to our gate, and I discovered that Amanda and I were not seated together, so I approached the agent with a request to change our seats. A few minutes later, the microphone clicked on and I heard the agent say, "Teegins party, please come to the desk." Everyone stared at us—suddenly the entire room of people knew that we had to be related to the tragedy they merely read about in the morning paper or watched in bits and pieces on the airport television screen.

Amanda and I held onto each other for most of the trip to Oklahoma City. Bill had suddenly been snatched from us. Who knew? Might something similar happen to one, or even to both of us also? Over and over, Amanda kept thanking Tony for driving her the 90 minutes from St. Cloud to Minneapolis and for trying to help her overcome her fear of flying, a long held fear that had now grown a thousand times stronger.

Everything had been hurry up and wait. Then suddenly, we were home—touching down to real life. We walked from the jet way into the open arms of dozens of friends with such sad faces. As I remember it, we said little—what could we say? Harry Goldsmith, who I worked with at the airport ticket counter for three years, who usually put up a tough front, wrapped his arms around me, kissed my cheek, and asked, "Are you ready for this? There's a lot of people waiting for you in the gate area."

KWTV President David Griffin and his wife, Kirsten, were there, along with Kelly and Teri Ogle, Richard and Sandy Marlin, Jon and Diane King , and many others. Amanda and I needed every person there. We needed their friendship, their steadying love, and their support. We were still in such a daze. We were unaware, until interviewing people for this book, that Jon and Diane King drove us home from the airport.

My brother, Jim, and his wife, Charlene were driving up from Colleyville, a suburb of Dallas. Bill's parents, his brother, and his sister were coming as quickly as they could from Amarillo. It would be so strange to face everyone in our home, for the first time without Bill. It was beginning to sink in that I was alone for the first time in 27 years.

I had no idea what it would be like to unlock our front door, knowing Bill would never walk through it again. I was afraid to walk into the house alone, scared to walk into the study where Bill's pipe lay in the ashtray, a bit of tobacco still in the bowl. Unthinking, I pinched some of it and slid it into my pocket.

I imagined Bill would surely walk into the room at any moment, tease us gently for our sorrow, our lack of faith, retire to his easy chair, puff on his favorite flavor— vanilla—an aroma that lingered in the room until I sold the house. I wanted to sink into that smell, so familiar, so comforting. I wanted to curl up in Bill's chair, not talk, not even think, just try to feel him there, one room away, just busy with something, momentarily out of my sight.

I threw my coat on our bed and stared at it. Our bed, the one we'd picked out together, paid for with money we had saved. The mattress was "just so," hard enough for Bill and soft enough for me, the bed where we slept together, where we made love.

I could not bring myself to walk into the closet full of Bill's beautiful wardrobe—suits, coats, and ties we had shopped for together. It was a painful reminder that this closet full of clothes was of no use to him any longer.

It hurt deeply to look out the back window at Bill's main retreat, the swimming pool he'd slip into, to wash away a tiring day, and his favorite mesh chair, where he read the daily newspaper and drank his morning coffee from the golf cup Amanda bought him for his 48th birthday.

I heard the chimes of the grandfather clock echo in the hallway. I heard the wind scraping tree limbs against the house. I heard my heels click across the cold, clean kitchen tile, but hard as I tried, I did not hear Bill's deep and memorable voice. Death is silence, a strange phenomenon, and one to which I still have not grown accustomed.

Sometime later, I wrote this poem which I dedicate to Bill, I call it "Brief Moment:"

Life's brief moment,
Silenced.
My love, laughter,
My all.
Changes deep,
Never sleep.
Transluscent memories,
Dreamer's dream,
Awaken, beautiful soul.
One brief moment
Is all I ask.
My love, laughter,
My all.

a tribute to BILL

BY JOHN ROHDE

(Two days after Bill died in the plane crash, John Rohde wrote about the OSU tragedy in the sky in his column in The Daily Oklahoman.*)*

The exact moment a plane crashed into a snow-covered field in Colorado on Saturday, the spirits of 10 people began to head skyward.

Presumably, sportscaster Bill Teegins handled the play-by-play of their ascent to heaven. And you can bet Teegins spoke of everyone but himself. He heaped praise upon Oklahoma State basketball players Nate Fleming and Daniel Lawson. He bragged about how well assistant media relations director Will Hancock did his job, and how well director of basketball operations Pat Noyes did his.

He was sure to mention the importance of trainer Bryan Luinstra, student assistant Jared Weiberg, and radio engineer Kendall Durfey. He shared the confidence he had in pilots Denver Mills and Bjorn Fahlstrom. But, not a single word about himself.

Teegins hated being the focus of any story, so he can feel free to hate this one. He did what the best in the business are supposed to do. He deflected attention away from himself and zeroed in on the topic at hand. He was modest, funny, self-deprecating, and quick with a compliment. Could there be a better combination?

The last person who wanted to talk about Teegins was Teegins himself. Ask him how his radio broadcast went and he'd habitually say, "Oh, it was the

usual. I got too excited. My voice cracked. I forgot to mention the score. I was terrible. Don't tell my boss, OK?"

In casual conversation, Teegins often did impersonations of OSU coach Eddie Sutton. Teegins would scan the Sutton Library and deliver each tale with a slow-paced drawl. It had gotten to the point where rather than say hello, Teegins would greet people in full Sutton mode, complete with a signature, "Oh, fercryinoutloud."

Teegins often did imperson- ations of OSU coach Eddie Sutton. It had gotten to the point where rather than say hello, Teegins would greet people in full Sutton mode, complete with a signature, "Oh, fercryinoutloud."

The last time I talked to Teegins was six days ago to offer congratulations. He had recently been named Oklahoma's sportscaster of the year for the eighth time. It gave me a chance to say, "Hey, congrats. Well-deserved. You stud." It gave Teegins a chance to change the topic.

Within 10 seconds, he had steered the conversation completely away from himself. He asked about my wife and son; dogged his beloved Minnesota Vikings for their pathetic performance against the New York Giants in the NFC championship game; spoke of the predictable improvement of the OSU basketball team, and said, "Coach Sutton is doing it again, isn't he?"

It was close to airtime when we spoke that day, so Teegins didn't have time to share a piece of baseball trivia. Thank goodness. His trivia questions made me feel so inept…

Janis and Amanda Teegins are finding out just how much their husband/father meant to so many people from so many places. All this attention is intended to help them, not hurt them.

Although he was the voice of the Cowboys, Teegins somehow transcended the bedlam of OU vs. OSU. This was no easy trick. Sutton loved him, yet so did Oklahoma basketball coach Kelvin Sampson.

Members of television, radio, and newspaper—who rarely agree on anything—agreed on Teegins.

KWTV-9…carried Super Bowl XXXV on Sunday. But throughout the state of Oklahoma and several places beyond, the passing of 10 friends dwarfed the biggest sporting event of the year. Teegins, a man who hated the spotlight, outshined the Super Bowl.

Flying in those pint-sized planes scared the wits out of Teegins. He kiddingly predicted a plane crash would be his demise someday, and it was.

"So Bill," former KWTV partner Chris Harrison remembers asking Teegins tongue-in-cheek, "how do you want us to say goodbye?" Teegins said, "Ah, just have a beer and tell a good story about me—if you can think of one."

We can think of many, but we need Teegins to do the play-by-play.

Come on, Teegs. Give us just one more trivia question. But keep it simple, OK?

> I am deeply sad-
> dened to hear of the
> tragedy that has hit
> the Oklahoma State
> University family.
>
> **OKLAHOMA
> GOVERNOR FRANK
> KEATING**

chapter 12

HEARTFELT RESPONSE

(O)klahomans' response to Bill's death was overwhelming. KWTV and I received thousands of cards, letters, and E-mails. Most were from strangers who had never met Bill, certainly had never met me, but felt he was like family because he came into their living rooms every night with such energy and enthusiasm in his words and his voice.

People from every corner of the state of Oklahoma and beyond offered their sympathy for Amanda and for me and for Bill's colleagues at KWTV. Some offered prayers, others lit candles in their homes in Bill's memory, and one catering company offered to provide food for our family's gatherings. A man from Marlow, Oklahoma, suggested creating a Bill Teegins Trophy for outstanding athletes. One caller recommended renaming the street in front of KWTV "Bill Teegins Boulevard." Many people expressed their shock, sadness, and support for us and I'd like to share some of their thoughts:

> I never met Bill, but he came into my living room almost every night. I never spoke with him, but his voice filled my truck every afternoon after work.
>
> > John Davidson
> > Oklahoma City

> Where Bill is now, he can watch every game from a front row seat, be a guardian angel for his wife and daughter, and still sit beside his colleagues during every newscast.
>
> > Mike Jennings
> > Oklahoma City

God's heaven shines brighter because of the light that Bill gave to us all on earth.

David Hodges
Oklahoma City

As my tears begin to flow, I just think to myself…Bill can now pick what beach he wants to lie on and be that beach bum he talked about being.

Kenny Bridgman
Lone Grove, Oklahoma

Bill's death feels personal to me. He came across as such a real person that it feels as if a dear friend has been lost. It doesn't seem fair that such a kind and sincere person should be taken away from a world where "good guys" seem to be in short supply.

Nancy Klos

I am stunned to realize how much I'll miss Bill. Since learning of his passing, I have shed countless tears when I recall his wit, his charm, the crinkle of his eyes, his love for baseball.

Anonymous

Oklahoma sports journalism has lost a crown jewel of the profession.

Frog

Although we did not know him personally, we have watched and listened to him for such a long time; that it seems as if we did. He brought the Oklahoma sports "home" in a professional and fun manner and his passing is a great loss.

The Osborne Family
McLoud, Oklahoma

In a way, we all knew Bill. He was in our homes every day, smiling, joking, and representing Oklahoma and Channel 9 with class, style, humor, and professionalism.

Cindy Burns
Oklahoma City

Oklahoma was given a gift, and the gift was Bill Teegins.

Ruth
Cordell, Oklahoma

Heaven must have needed a great sportscaster to call the game tomorrow.

Kevin Richter
Enid, Oklahoma[1]

Public officials from all across the state sent words of comfort. Governor Frank Keating and First Lady Cathy Keating said they were "shocked and saddened."[2] Oklahoma City Mayor Kirk Humphreys said, "This tragedy cannot take from you the love, the memories, and the joy Bill brought to your lives."[3] Congressman, J.C. Watts, Jr., said, "We will miss the warmth, compassion, and humor that Bill brought to our lives."[4] United States Senator Don Nickles and so many others sent expressions of comfort.

United States Senator Jean Carnahan, of Missouri, who had lost her husband and son in a recent small airplane crash, wrote these words to me, "Be assured that God does mend the heart slowly, but surely. Rely on friends, family, and faith. They do make a difference. You are borne through the day on the wings of prayer by more people than you will ever know."[5]

"This is just terrible," said Bill Self, who grew up in Edmond, played basketball at OSU, and then became head coach at the University of Illinois. Bill continued, "You have the bombing, the tornado, and now this. How much more can the state endure?"[6]

Our friend Bob Losure expressed his grief by choosing to remember Bill in the early days at KOTV, singing along with Marvin Gaye and Tammi Terrell to the tune "Ain't no mountain high enough...ain't no valley low enough...to keep me away from you."[7]

Kate Sandefur, whose father-in-law, Eric Sandefur, had been Bill's good friend since the eighth grade, said, "I cannot even imagine the pain you are going through. Our family is forever saddened by your loss."[8]

The headline on Berry Tramel's column in *The Daily Oklahoman* two days after the crash read, "OSU WILL BE FOREVER CHANGED BY TRAGEDY." Berry wrote:

A cold rain fell Sunday on a campus awash in tears. When the skies clear, when the grief subsides, left will be a school changed. Oklahoma State University will never be the same...Ten good men died Saturday night, one time zone west, when a diving plane crashed, ripping a hole not just in a frozen field, but in the heart of a tight-knit school.[9]

Bill's friend, Bob Hersom, in his *Oklahoman* column, pointed out that Bill was 48 years old but acted younger and looked younger. Bob recited a memory from the Big 12 basketball tournament in Kansas City the year before. He wrote, "Maybe a dozen of us media types were holding court in a restaurant near Kemper Arena," he wrote. "I noticed a couple at a small table off to the side. They were oblivious to the crowd, obviously enjoying each other's thoughts. "The next day, Bob told Bill that he had been genuinely impressed to see that Bill and I were still acting like newlyweds after more than twenty years of marriage.[10]

OSU fans were particularly hard hit by the tragedy, and they expressed their sadness by telephone, E-mail, cards, letters, and in person at every opportunity. Complete strangers came up to me in the grocery store with tears in their eyes, asking how they could help and telling me how much they also missed Bill. Jeff Barker, an OSU basketball fan, E-mailed me, "I am in great pain, knowing I will never hear the voice of an excited Bill Teegins say, 'Mo Baker for three...HE GOT IT!'"[11]

Pat Door, a longtime accounting professor at OSU, remembers talking to Bill at basketball games. She said what so many others, in one way or another, said, "Bill had that special way of making you feel that you and what you had to say was very important to him."[12]

The grief was not limited to just OSU fans. John Gilbert wrote, "I am an Oklahoma Sooner fan that is Boomer Sooner through and through. However, after the news of this awful tragedy, I feel compelled to hang an OSU banner next to my OU banner because we are not Sooners or Cowboys—we are Oklahomans, grieving Oklahomans."[13]

Andy Stewart was a six-year-old in Duncan who adored Bill. For Christmas, his aunt asked Bill for an autographed photograph. Across the lower corner, Bill had written, "To Andy, my #1 fan in Duncan. Thanks for watching! Bill Teegins." When his parents told him that Bill was dead, the youngster said, "At least I can always remember him, can't I Mom?"[14]

Dan Royal, who had worked with Bill in Amarillo in the late 1970s, wrote, "I would like to think that at this moment, Bill is pestering Babe Ruth for obscure stats and checking the ESPN schedule."[15]

Sadness inspired people to turn to reflection through written words. Friends and fans sent hundreds of poems about Bill's sudden death. Since

I enjoy writing, the fact that people who never knew Bill took the time to put their feelings of compassion and sadness into rhyme, and looping, lovely free verse, made me feel so loved. I can still sit and cry when I pull out and read those poems. Here are excerpts from a few of them:

Will Bill Teegins be missed?
"For cryin' out loud!"
Would the rising and setting of the sun be missed?
Would the warm spring rains be missed?
Would the cool breeze on a hot summer day be missed?
Would the beauty of a fresh fallen snow be missed?
Would the heavens miss the singing of the angels?
Will Bill Teegins be missed?
"For cryin' out loud!"

Caylon Berglan

We all share thousands of tears,
Because we care
Now you are in heaven calling the shots,
You were a slam-dunk, Bill,
In all our hearts.

Angela Mayabb

"Hi everybody!" – will be missed
By the TV/radio crowds;
We could also count on you to say,
"Ah, c'mon, fer cryin' out loud!"

James Cudd

He shared with us many a funny line.
With a wink of his eye, we knew things were fine.

June C. Kelly

Night after night, that's how we met,
Sitting at that desk, on my TV set.
Information and trivia in your head was stored,
Always on top of all the sports and who scored.
You had a smile that won the state,
And a personality no one could hate.

Always smiling and telling jokes,
You won the hearts of many folks.
At our desk you will sit no more.
For up in heaven, you're in charge of God's final score.

Donna Hanson

Oklahoma has lost its voice,
Someone else made the call; it wasn't his choice.
All of Oklahoma will shed some tears,
For he put the "Ump" in sports for over 13 years.
His style has graced our lives since '87,
Now he will be doing Play by Play in Heaven.

K.C. Brett[16]

Cowboy poet Baxter Black penned a beautiful poem to memorialize the 10 men lost in the crash:

The Lord spoke to the heavy hearts that stood with hats in hand
"Your sadness pains me deeply and I know you'll miss these men
But, it's true what you've been hearing, Heaven is a real place."…
It's the ranch they've always dreamed of and never knew they'd find
And if you think about, you can see it in your mind.
Them, leanin' in their saddles with their ol' hats on their heads,
Contentment set upon their faces like blankets on their beds.[17]

ESPN sportscaster Bob Carpenter, who had been Bill's competitor in the 1980s when they were both in Tulsa, was deeply touched by the tragedy. The night after the crash, he flew to Salt Lake City, Utah, to call the Utah-Brigham Young University basketball game. There, he, and ESPN partner Jimmy Dykes, decided to contact OSU and volunteer to broadcast the remaining televised OSU basketball games, and donate their pay to the families of those killed in the crash. Tom Dirato accepted their kind offer and sealed the deal the next day.[18]

Condolences also came from hundreds of people outside of Oklahoma. Jim Hagedorn, a sailor on board the USS *Carl Vinson*, had been stationed at Tinker Air Force Base. He wrote, "Bill became part of my day, as I am a sports fanatic. Traveling all over the world, I have never seen a more upbeat and professional man. I know the folks of Oklahoma will wrap their arms around Bill's family."[19]

Jeff Cheap was an OSU graduate from Woodward, Oklahoma, living and teaching in Beijing, China, when he learned of the plane crash on the Internet. He felt helpless being so far away. To honor Bill and the others, he wore his OSU sweatshirt to teach his classes. He wrote this note to me, "I have made sure that all the other teachers and students here know that these are not just names in the news, but real people, great people, and that this is a huge loss for everyone."[20]

From New Orleans, Louisiana, came an E-mail from a man identified only as "D. Irish," who was "deeply saddened" by the news. He said, "My children grew up watching Bill. It was like losing a member of our own family."[21]

The loss wasn't limited to sports fans, as a man named Mike talked about how his wife, "never a big sports fan," would sit with him and watch sports when Bill came on the air. "She just loved to hear the comments Bill threw in after a short segment aired—he was so straightforward and humorous," Mike said. Another came from a woman who wrote, "I am not a sports fan, but I was a fan of Bill. I will always remember his smile— it was contagious."[22]

Truly, Bill had a way of transcending sports and making a lasting impression on people. In the days following the crash, it helped to know this, to know, to hear, to see and to realize that I would never stand alone mourning this man whom I loved—A love I've found that I still share with many family, friends, and admirers of "our" Bill.

a tribute to BILL

BY KELVIN SAMPSON

I n my years as the men's basketball coach at the University of Oklahoma, I have worked with many great people from all walks of life. But Bill Teegins was a man who transcended the profession of which he was part—the media. Bill wasn't just a sportscaster, radio commentator, television show host, or sports anchor—he was the best I have ever worked with.

His life is best described by the words of Ralph Waldo Emerson, "Do not go where the path may lead, go instead where there is no path, and leave a trail."

Bill spent his lifetime devoted to his family and his profession—sports. He left a valuable legacy for others to follow—treat everyone as human beings and treat them fairly and with great respect.

When Bill hosted my television show, he made my job very easy. He had a gift from God to make everyone around him better. It has been said that sports is a great metaphor for life's more difficult lessons. Bill lived his life in a way that we all can be proud and be honored to have known him. What a great legacy to leave behind!

> I walked around greeting friends and family, making funeral plans, and all the while my heart was breaking. I was overwhelmed and suffocating in grief, and missing Bill so terribly.
>
> **JANIS TEEGINS**

chapter 13

THE
EMPTY CHAIR

*T*he week following Bill's death, the phone rang constantly—flowers and plants lined our living room and extended down the hall and into the kitchen. Casseroles, hams, and baked goods arrived in a steady stream, and friends and family let us know their arrival times, their flight numbers, and how many hours they thought it would take to drive. Some traveled from as far away as California, Tennessee, Ohio, and Minnesota to offer their love and support to Amanda and me, each trying to say the right words and offering whatever help they could think of in our time of grief.

Chad, our lawn keeper, came by and didn't even knock—he just started sprucing up the yard. I went outside to thank him and he said it was the only thing he could think of to do to help us. The same thing happened with the housekeeper and the pool man. It was if all the angels who commonly, quietly, stepped into the corners of our life and worked their magic to keep us presentable and moving forward, now knew, instinctively, that we needed them more than ever. One of our neighbors, an Oklahoma City police officer, stopped by to say not to worry, that he and other officers would be watching our home while our family attended the funeral. The Oklahoma Highway Patrol escorted our family to Tulsa for the graveside service. The outpouring of love from Oklahomans continued, and still continues to amaze me.

As expected, Oklahoma newspapers and radio and television stations devoted an incredible amount of space and time to the story. The day after the plane crash was Super Bowl Sunday, one of the biggest sports days of the year. To begin the Sunday night newscast on KWTV, Jenifer Reynolds pointed to the empty chair beside co-anchor Kelly Ogle and in an emotion filled voice said, "Tonight we're missing a beloved member of our News 9 family who no doubt would be right here in the middle of it all."[1]

The newscasts on Channel 9 that night turned into a tribute to Bill. Alex Cameron, his cheeks chaffed from the cold blustery wind, reported from the empty field in Colorado where National Transportation Safety Board investigators had placed small, colored flags, marking the location of "evidence" at the crash scene. Kelly Ogle and Jenifer Reynolds shared their emotional sadness with viewers, and at various stopping points in the Super Bowl, they read E-mails from people who shared their same sense of excruciating loss.

For the first time in three years, the Bill and Dean sports report was just Dean Blevins, who began, "This chair is empty and will…forever be empty. I lose my partner, Bill Teegins, and you lose a friend at home. But Amanda loses a daddy and Janis loses a loving husband."[2]

Dean gave the lopsided score in the Super Bowl, a sporting event that, because of the tragedy, had seemingly lost its luster. Then, he launched into a personal tribute to Bill. He even talked about the special wink that Bill gave him when an interview was going great or his team was playing its best.[3]

I saw that wink first, I wanted to say. It had been our ritual for at least the past 10 years, at the start of each OSU home basketball game. Bill would look into the arena where I always sat and gave me his wink and reassuring grin, his signal that he knew that I was there—that it mattered to him that I'd made it safely to the game and would be watching it all, watching him.

Dean showed videotape of Bill calling a football game, a basketball game, and overseeing some of the greatest Oklahoma sporting events. He interviewed former OSU football coaches Bob Simmons and Pat Jones.

"Bill was a good guy and excellent journalist," Pat said. Kelvin Sampson, OU men's basketball coach added, "Bill was a selfless person who tried to make everyone else look good."[4]

In a unique display of how much the KWTV sports family loved Bill, the remaining five members of the sports department gathered extemporaneously with Dean on the set. Greg Kerr, in a broken voice, recounted the extra 90 minutes he had spent with Bill the previous Thursday night while covering a Southern Nazarene University basketball game. As he began to cry before living rooms full of equally tearful watchers, he said, "It wasn't anything out of the norm, but today I'm thankful that we did it."[5]

Sports reporter Jeff Losh, whose family, ironically, owned the field in Colorado where the plane crashed, talked about Bill as a teacher and mentor, as almost a father figure. "In church today it occurred to me that Bill is still teaching me, and all of us, another lesson," Jeff said. "That lesson is—to have faith, and to believe in God and Jesus and to know that Bill and the other nine are in heaven right now."[6]

Producer Toby Roland, who spent 60 to 70 hours a week with Bill, said, "Bill was equally as genuine a person in real life as he was across the camera. It was impossible to meet Bill Teegins and not like him. It was equally impossible to know Bill Teegins and not love the man."[7]

I sat in Bill's chair in our den listening to these words, while various family members were still about, still walking through these early empty hours with Amanda and me. It pained me deeply, seeing Bill's friends and colleagues in sorrow and grief, sharing the same love and hurt over the loss of Bill that I felt. Helpless and hopeless, knowing that there was nothing anyone could really do, I listened to their words, and suddenly I saw how far Bill's life, young as he was, had already gone. I listened to their words and I knew that they were all true.

Dean closed the newscast by calling Bill a man of principle, God, family, and friends. "So, as long as we are lucky enough to be on this side of the grass," he said, "may we learn from the life of our friend, Bill Teegins. Let us live, let us hope, and let us love. Goodnight Bill."[8]

KWTV President David Griffin held a "family" meeting of Channel 9 employees. He offered counseling services to those who needed them and urged Bill's fellow employees to write notes and funny stories about Bill so that Amanda and I would have them for a scrapbook. He invited Pastor Pete Balaban of Edmond's Peace Lutheran Church to pray and to preside over a moment of silence for Bill. As a final gesture, David handed out Minnesota Twins baseball cards that the owners of the Old Ball Park in Oklahoma City had given to David's wife, Kirsten, for the occasion.[9]

As a closing to the meeting, David said, "This is the toughest thing we've gone through. But remember, Bill would want us all to take care of ourselves and to make sure that we show our love to our families."[10]

On Sunday night, Coach Eddie Sutton telephoned me at home and told me how much Bill had meant to him. He called Bill "a marvelous man," and he said that if he could have ever had a brother, he would have wanted it to be Bill.

On Wednesday, January 31, 2001, 13,000 mourners filled Gallagher-Iba Arena as a show of respect for the 10 men lost in the plane crash four days earlier. As the memorial service at OSU began, bells tolled across the OU campus in Norman, 100 miles away. This was a unique show of solidarity between the state's two largest universities.

As the limousine carrying our family members pulled into the parking lot the arena, everyone in the long, black car grew quiet, solemn, each of us trying, it seemed, to gather ourselves, to muster enough strength and courage to get through this ceremony. OSU had assigned counselors, administrators, or faculty members to greet and walk with each family. OSU Associate Athletic Director/Director of Media Relations, Steve Buzzard, and his sweet wife, Cathy, walked Amanda and me to the arena.

Steve held my arm, made sure I was steady, and shared the same pulse of dread and loss with Amanda and me. Tears rolled down all our cheeks as we silently walked from the parking lot to the room reserved for the families of the victims. Steve had been instrumental in hiring Bill as Voice of the Cowboys and they had become close friends over the years. I was comforted that he and Cathy chose to walk with us.

As we entered the room, everyone was given a teddy bear dressed in OSU orange and black. It felt good to have something soft and safe to hold close, to grasp onto. It was overwhelming to see the room packed with hundreds of people who were all affected by the loss of a loved one in the tragedy. Shortly, we would be escorted beyond the safety and isolation of that room, into an arena of life that I'm pretty sure none of us had ever known before.

The newly rebuilt Gallagher-Iba Arena had been dedicated just three weeks before. Bill had told me about it, how much he liked what they'd done, but I didn't dream that the first time I would see the new arena would be to attend a memorial service for the man I loved.

This day, the usual smell of popcorn was replaced with the strong bouquet of the hundreds of flowers which had been brought to the memorial service by students, fans, and members of the community who were affected by the same tragic loss I felt. The normal sound of basketballs bouncing off wooden floors and the deafening roar of cheers and boos was replaced with a deep, aching quiet.

The families of the victims sat at court level, and I found myself looking up into the stands, a vantage point that the players saw every game. Only this time, I was in the game, a game I never wanted to play, looking into the tear-filled eyes, the wounded faces of all those people who gave up their afternoon to pay their last respects for these 10 men. A makeshift stage at the north end of the arena sat behind large framed pictures of the 10 fallen Cowboys. I sat through the ceremony in quiet disbelief, my eyes blurred with tears, telling myself over and over, "This can't be so."

Near the end of the ceremony, the Spirit Band gently played the OSU Alma Mater Hymn as the crowd held arms, and sang softly, in unison, swaying side to side:

Proud and immortal,
Bright shines your name;
   Oklahoma State,
We herald your fame
Ever you'll find us—
   loyal and true.
To our Alma Mater.
    O—S—U

It was if the huge crowd was trying to give the families a big hug.

I heard the wonderful words spoken about Bill and the others, but I could not really listen. All I could do was gaze at Bill's portrait, the truth, the sad sick truth slowly sinking into me as steadily as did the cold of the day once we stepped outside the arena.

The enormity of the loss was summed up best by *The Daily Oklahoman* reporter Jay C. Grelen, "The 10 men who died left five wives without husbands, eight daughters and two sons without fathers, mothers and fathers without sons, 12 siblings without brothers, and one fiancée."[11]

Kelly Ogle presided over the service, which was a mix of somber memories and humorous stories. Other speakers included Governor Frank Keating, OSU President James Halligan, OSU Vice President Harry Birdwell, and Lieutenant Governor Mary Fallin. Few eyes were dry during the service.

The huge crowd that attended the memorial service at Gallagher-Iba Arena in Stillwater the Wednesday following the crash. "Let us resolve that we shall never forget them," OSU President James Halligan said. *Courtesy* Tulsa World.

10 REMEMBERED

A window sticker to honor the 10 victims of the OSU plane crash. Our close family and friends still carry a key chain with Bill's photograph on one side and, on the other side, the famous Grantland Rice quote, "For when the One Great Scorer comes to write against your name, He marks—not that you won or lost—but how you played the game."

Near the end of the ceremony, President Halligan announced that OSU would provide for the education of all surviving children and would participate in the building of a memorial at the site of the crash near Strasburg, Colorado.

The memorial service was broadcast live on seven television stations in Oklahoma, by Fox Sports Southwest, and nationally by ESPNews. The only audible reaction by the audience during the moving service was when Kelly introduced Coach Sutton. He was given a gentle, respectful 20-second standing ovation.[12]

Coach Sutton told the crowd, "In dealing with death, nothing seems more confusing, more senseless, more jolting, than when the light goes out far too soon on bright young lives." Of Bill, Coach said, "He was the most humble sportscaster I've ever known. I've never met any sportscaster or sportswriter who didn't like Bill. He always had a big smile for me."[13]

RIGHT: This full-page tribute to Bill was purchased by KWTV for the back cover of the basketball program at Gallagher-Iba Arena. At the first basketball game after Bill's death, Janis and Amanda sat near courtside. When they looked up into the crowd, there saw thousands of the tributes, as fans opened their programs. It was a poignant reminder of the great loss they had just suffered. *Courtesy Oklahoma State University.*

In Loving Memory

Bill Teegins
1952-2001

Our friend, colleague, and valued member of our team.

We Miss You.

Our hearts go out to all of the families and friends who lost a loved one in the OSU Tragedy.

After the public displays of honor and respect for Bill and the other nine victims were winding down, it came time for me to tackle the toughest assignment of my life—to finish the arrangements I'd begun the week before while scribbling notes on the backs of Christmas napkins in a lonely Boston apartment. Now it was time to attend the funeral for the one love of my life.

We were overwhelmed, yet thankful, for the generosity of our friends and neighbors. There was a constant stream of meals in the Tietgens' kitchen and we quickly ran out of room in the refrigerator. Since it was winter and the temperature was cold outside, we started stacking casseroles and baked goods on the tops and trunks of cars in our garage. My sisters-in-law, Paula Cole and Audrey Tietgens, ran the kitchen, serving and organizing meals for the large number of family and friends who flooded our home during that first week following the accident. Carol Tietgens, Bill's mother, helped with clean up and kept a list of names of people who brought food. My brothers-in-law, David Cole and Scott Tietgens, answered the door and the frequently ringing phone, and helped me with too many plans and errands to mention. I am so grateful to each of them.

During this whole time, our close friends, Jon and Diane King, offered our entire family their tears, memories, love and support, occasionally even getting us laughing. Good friends, Sandy and Richard Marlin, bought us a fax machine for all of the business transactions that would be necessary to take care of in the coming months. Various members of our TV-9 family came by often to check on us and remind us how much they cared—never for a minute did we doubt that.

One morning, my brother Jim and his wife Charlene drove to the funeral home and began the task of making arrangements for me, narrowing the choices, so that it would be a quick and less painful process for me. I'll never forget the thoughtfulness and love they showed me in that gesture.

We chose to have Bill's service on Friday, February 2, at the First Baptist Church in Edmond, since its sanctuary was much larger than our home church, Lord of Life Lutheran Church, also in Edmond. Susie Stussi, a friend from our church, helped co-ordinate the family reception that was held in the fellowship hall following the service. A group of women from First Baptist volunteered to set up and serve coffee, donuts, and cookies that were provided by our friend, Mark Godwin, who at that time, owned several grocery stores in Edmond.

Dr. Alan Day, pastor of First Baptist Church, was open to any ideas we had for the service, and he even allowed Channel 9 to set up a sound system in the fellowship hall so that Bill's voice, announcing a previous OSU game, could be played quietly during the reception. Lord of Life's interim pastor, Ben Veit had been at our church only a short time when he and Bishop Floyd Schoenhals, bishop of the Arkansas Oklahoma Synod and close family friend, held service for more than 1,800 mourners.

We arrived early and our family gathered in a separate room so we could collect ourselves, give each other encouragement, and then enter the sanctuary as a group. Barry Switzer, former head football coach at OU, made it a point to find me and give me a hug as the two of us shared quiet tears for Bill. Many other people came that day and showed their admiration and respect for Bill.

Governor Frank Keating opened the service saying, "Whether we like sports or whether we even watch TV, here was a warm, endearing, decent, wonderful human being who has made our world a better place."[14] Greg Blackwood choked back tears and said, "Today, I miss a friend…Bill, I love you, and I miss you."[15]

Kelly Ogle paid tribute to Bill's faith when he said, "If we believe in his Lord and Savior, Jesus Christ, we will get to see him again and I just can't wait to see what he's cooking up for me right now."[16]

Jenifer Reynolds said she would miss Bill walking the halls of Channel 9 snapping his fingers, practicing his golf swing while he waited for the copy machine to warm up. Jenifer shared how she would miss hearing Bill's patented microphone check, too, "This is the test of the Jamochian Broadcasting Network."[17]

"If Bill were here today," Gary England told the attendees, "he would say, "For cryin' out loud, these people should be at work."[18]

Greg Kerr related how Bill would never say goodbye in a telephone conversation—he'd just say, "See you tomorrow." Greg said, "You know, I'm glad he never said goodbye, because in my heart, he never will."[19]

OSU broadcast director and producer Joe Riddle told stories of Bill doing Eddie Sutton imitations and how he nearly got them thrown off the plane for home on several road trips. Joe remembered when he himself had been a young radio reporter and how Bill remembered his name after meeting him just once. "He had courtesy and respect and was always a gentleman to everyone around him," Joe said.[20]

To all these words, all these expressions of love for Bill, I sat there numb, but proud, thinking one thing, "Yes."

Lieutenant Governor Fallin presented Amanda and me the Oklahoma flag that had flown at half-staff over the Capitol the day before. Then, Pastor Veit read lessons that Amanda and I had suggested, lessons of the great love of God and Jesus Christ that had wrapped Bill in his life from its beginning to end. Pastor Veit said, "Because of God's grace and love and forgiveness, Bill Teegins was free to be hopeful and helpful. He was free to live and love life to the fullest, as he did, and to be a servant of God for others. What you and I saw in Bill Teegins was the spirit of Jesus Christ living in him and through him."[21]

Following the service, we took Bill to his final resting place at Floral Haven Cemetery in Broken Arrow, Oklahoma. It is a beautiful cemetery where both my parents had been buried several years earlier. Watching all the cars following us that long distance, watching everyone being so unwilling to go home yet, to let go of the day, gave me a sense of comfort and calm. Despite my deep sadness, I felt the love of Bill and all our friends and family that day. I feel it still.

a tribute to BILL

BY JENIFER REYNOLDS

His voice and his laugh are, unquestionably, the things I miss most about Bill. When they were suddenly gone, it was as if a light had gone out—on the set, in the newsroom, in our lives. Even now, as I write this, I can hear his laugh ringing in my mind and it makes me smile. Bill laughed often, almost as much as he made us laugh.

I still can't help but chuckle when I remember the night Dean Blevins' flip-flop slipped off the rung of his chair and smacked the floor with what sounded like a gunshot just as they started a sportscast. Both men jumped and Dean sheepishly told Bill, "You should never wear thongs on the air" to which Bill responded without a pause, "At least not on your feet." I laughed so hard I spit Diet Dr. Pepper all over the anchor desk, but Bill went on with the next sports story and never missed a beat.

I remember the night we had reported on a fire at a local elementary school during the 10:00 p.m. newscast. We were recapping the story at the end of the broadcast, and, trying to use up the 20 seconds we had left, I said, "We don't know if they'll be able to have school tomorrow, so it might be a good idea for parents to call before they take the kids in." We said goodnight and the newscast ended. Then, Gary England turned to me and said, "JR, this is June. There won't be school tomorrow." I was mortified. Kelly Ogle tried to make me feel better by pointing out some kids might have summer classes. Bill said,

"Yeah, but tomorrow is SATURDAY." I was so embarrassed my face went crimson and my ears were ringing, but I couldn't help laughing when Bill launched into his best over-dramatic broadcast voice and announced, "So for all you kids in Saturday, summer school, call before you go in tomorrow!"

It was the same voice he used each night when the audio operators asked for a microphone check to which he invariably responded, "This is a test, not intended for actual broadcast use. Come in, Tokyo…" Whenever anything went wrong on the air, he would use the same voice to mimic what he always said was his future in the business— broadcasting junior high basketball games on the public access channel in Tucumcari, New Mexico. It was the same voice he used each time he greeted co-anchor Angela Buckelew in the hall, with his patented "Hello, Angela BuckeLOOOO."

In the days that followed Bill's death, I realized how empty our world sounded without that voice and that laugh. I worried I would forget the sound of them over time—but I haven't. They are a gift he left behind for all of us who loved him. An even greater gift is knowing, when you look to the heavens, somewhere Bill is laughing still.

As it says in one of my favorite books, *The Little Prince*:

> In one of the stars I shall be living. In one of them I shall be laughing. And it will be as if all the stars are laughing when you look at the sky at night … You—only you—will have stars that can laugh!

> So now you'll understand if—on some crystal clear Oklahoma night—you see me look up at the stars, throw back my head, and laugh.

I couldn't help laughing when Bill launched into his best over-dramatic broadcast voice and announced, "So for all you kids in Saturday, summer school, call before you go in tomorrow!"

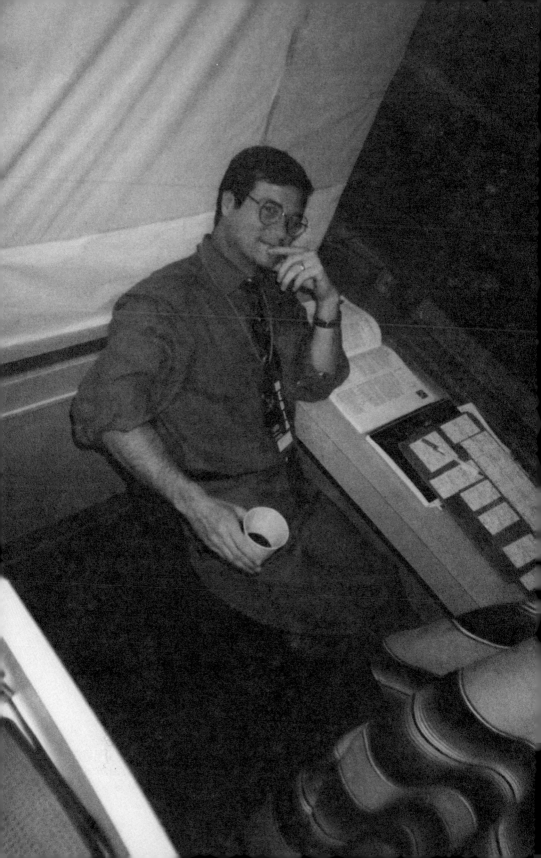

a tribute to

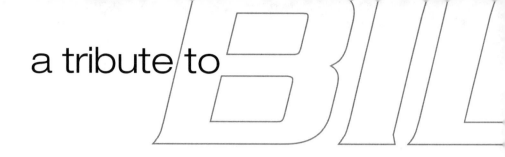

BY JON KING

The telephone would ring at our house and on the other end was that distinctive voice, familiar to nearly everyone in Oklahoma. For sure, it was the voice of our favorite person to find on the answering machine, "Hi Kings, this is Bill. Would you like go to dinner with us Saturday night?" Or, he'd say, "Hi Kings, it's Billy, can Jonnie come out to play?"

When the Air Force moved us to Oklahoma, we met Bill, Janis, and Amanda at Lord of Life Lutheran Church in Edmond. Bill, a greeter the first morning we attended, introduced himself, and instantly made my wife Diane and I feel we had found the church we wanted to attend.

Our friendship developed quickly through church, softball games, parties, and similar interests. Janis and Diane were both flight attendants and I shared Bill's intense love of sports. Soon, the four of us were doing something together every weekend.

A typical Saturday night with the Teegins included dinner at one of our favorite restaurants, a walk through Bricktown, relaxing by the pool, or playing a game of Trivial Pursuit. Bill easily answered all sports and history questions, but Janis and Diane used what Bill called "creative card selection"—they cheated—to keep pace with Bill and me.

Bill never considered himself a celebrity, but he was. Everywhere he went in Oklahoma, he was recognized. OSU fans wanted the latest news about their beloved Cowboys, and Sooner fans,

although they teasingly ribbed him, had a great respect for Bill. I marveled at how he always made time for anyone who approached him.

Bill loved to travel, to get away from it all. That led to the Teegins' and Kings' first vacation together—New Orleans. What a fun and exciting time we had eating gourmet food, gambling on the river boats, and enjoying the relaxed atmosphere of the French Quarter.

California was our next venture. We headed for the Sierra Foothills and some fantastic Zinfandel wines. While driving to Lake Tahoe, we found an oldies station on the radio and Bill knew the words and artist for almost every song. The four of us sang a little off key and laughed all the way to Tahoe. We had fun gambling, and, especially when Bill played, the Nevada economy became richer for it. Bill didn't care—he was on vacation and free from the pressures and daily grind of television sports casting.

As we re-entered San Francisco and drove across the Bay Bridge, Bill's interest in sports and history clicked in. Bill loved baseball parks, so we drove past Candlestick Park and Pacific Bell Park, the new home of the Giants. I wish they had been in town, because we would have been there, too.

Fisherman's Wharf, Golden Gate Bridge, Sausalito, Alcatraz, and then, the scenic vineyards and mountains of the Sonoma and Napa Valleys. What a perfect, fun-filled vacation. We spent our last night at a beautiful bed and breakfast in Calistoga, California. Bill awakened early, walked into town and bought his usual two or three newspapers, sat down with his coffee in hand, and was in seventh heaven.

Bill and I got to take two short trips together— Las Vegas, with four other Oklahoma City friends, and a mini-vacation to Chicago for a Cub's game at Wrigley Field. Bill loved Wrigley Field, smack in the middle of a residential area, loaded with nostalgia and baseball history. When we walked up the ramp of the stadium, our bellies full of burgers and beer, and saw those ivy covered outfield walls, Bill was like a kid in a candy store.

He drug me to every corner of the stadium pointing to various positions on the field and naming a player who'd done something impressive right

When we walked up the ramp of the stadium, our bellies full of burgers and beer, and saw those ivy covered outfield walls, Bill was like a kid in a candy store.

there…and right there…and…He knew all the player's batting averages, home run and pitching records—he was incredible. Afterward, during dinner at Mike Ditka's restaurant, we made a pact to see as many major league ballparks as possible. Fenway Park in Boston would be our next—we never got to Fenway.

On that fateful night in January of 2001, Diane and I had gone to the Miss University of Central Oklahoma Pageant. Driving home, we listened to music instead of the news. When we pulled into our driveway, our neighbors, the Dearduff's, immediately came over to see if we'd heard about the missing OSU plane—did we know that Bill was thought to have been one of the passengers?

I flew F-4's in Vietnam, and the day before one of my very dear friends was to return to the United States, he left on what was to have been his last mission. He never came back, and I had to be the one to tell our squadron the grim news. From the time we heard of the missing OSU plane, standing outside in the suddenly very cold driveway, it felt eerily the same—somehow I knew that my buddy Bill wasn't coming home either.

Later that night, when I talked to Janis, she asked me to confirm for her if it was really true. I told her, "Yes," but I remember nothing else about our conversation.

The next day, we met Janis and Amanda at the airport and drove them home. There lying on the floor, where he kept his game boards and brief-case, was Bill's un-used commercial airline ticket to Colorado. I'm not sure why Bill didn't take that ticket with him, but I do know Bill hated those small airplanes and, suddenly, standing in the room where we'd had so many fun evenings, I did too.

I never had a brother, but if I had, I would have wanted him to be exactly like Bill. He was fun, sincere, loyal, and had an unparalleled zest for life. I am a richer man for having known him.

To this day, when the phone rings, I still catch myself hoping that it's that unique and familiar voice on the other end, because, "Jonnie so wants to come out and play."

> Death is bitter—but he who is gone wants his lover to go on, to live on, to remember the good times, and cherish his memory.

HENRY WADSWORTH LONGFELLOW

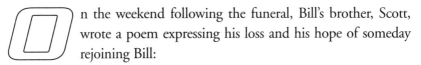

chapter 14

GOING ON

*O*n the weekend following the funeral, Bill's brother, Scott, wrote a poem expressing his loss and his hope of someday rejoining Bill:

O Lord, hear us as we pray
Give us strength for another day
Courage for the days ahead
And rest when we lay down in bed
Some days they seem so long
But I know we must go on
Give us comfort in our time of loss
Thank you for going to the cross
Because of that it's not goodbye
So dry the tears from our eyes
Together again, I know we will
So, I will see ya soon, my brother Bill.

In the early weeks after the crash, we all attempted to return to some sort of normalcy in our lives, even though that felt nearly impossible without Bill. A few days after the funeral, when the first roar of things seemed to be settling down, an eerie quiet came over our house. Bill's parents suggested that Amanda and I go home with them to Amarillo for a while. We desperately needed rest and we also needed help with writing thank-you notes for the huge numbers of flowers, letters, poems, and books we received from so many kind, good hearted people. We readily packed and went. We stayed for about a week, and it seemed to help, getting us away from the daily media coverage that continued back home in Oklahoma City.

Etched in my memory is the long sad drive coming home from Amarillo. I had never noticed the length of the trip or the barrenness of much of the landscape when I'd made the trip with Bill, or even when I had made the trip alone in Bill's Chrysler 300M. This time it was all so bleak, all so obvious.

Early in the trip, my hands picked up the smell of Bill's cologne that lingered on the leather wrapped steering wheel. Even though we were tired, as Amanda and I drew closer to home, neither one of us wanted to be there, neither of us wanted to unlock that door and step inside. I wanted to keep going, to keep driving on, maybe even forever, anything to not go home to that empty house, anything to ignore the harsh reality that awaited us.

I've heard of widows who did keep driving. It must be a common emotion at a time like that. But we did not keep going. We pulled into the garage with Bill's cologne smell still triggering bittersweet memories. I remember sitting in the dark garage several minutes before gathering the courage to unload the car and go inside. I knew two things—memories were all I had left—and I would sell Bill's car.

OSU resumed its basketball schedule on February 4, beating Missouri at Gallagher-Iba Arena in Stillwater. Thousands of fans must have noted the absence of their favorite play-by-play man because they scribbled incredible prayers, Bible verses, and very sweet notes on the huge, white, paper covered walls OSU had set up in the corridor outside the arena. OSU hoped that these messages would allow people to express their grief over the loss of the 10 men who died in the crash, and to convey their love and support to the families and friends left behind.

I can only speak for Amanda and me—but the contributions of each in his or her own small way did help. Many in the crowd, including coaches from both schools, wore orange ribbons in memory of the victims.

Coach Sutton called the game the most important coaching job of his career. He said, "It was important because it continues the healing process that all of us are going through."[1]

Learfield Sports, the company that owned the rights to the OSU games, came up with the excellent idea of having announcers for the Big 12 teams fill in for Bill as the play-by-play announcer on basketball broadcasts for the remainder of the season. The talent fee that normally would have gone to the individual announcers was matched by Learfield and donated to the Bill Teegins Fund at OSU.

When OU played the Cowboys in Stillwater on Valentine's Day, Amanda and I were present when John Morris, Baylor University's play-by-play announcer, filled in for Bill. A fan brought flowers with orange ribbons for the media sitting on press row. OU players wore orange t-shirts during warm-up that said, "We Remember," along with the names of the 10 victims on the back. After the game, Joe Riddle introduced Amanda and me to John, who was misty-eyed when he told us how honored he was to have sat in for Bill. "You will never know how many people are praying for you and the other families since the accident," he said.[2]

In February of 2001, just weeks after the crash, Bill's sister, Paula Cole and her husband, David, called to say they were driving to Denver for their daughter Jenna's volleyball tournament. They invited Amanda and me to join them, specifically to view the crash site, since they would be in the area. I couldn't bring myself to do that so soon after the accident, but Amanda and her close friend, Erica Smith, drove 12 hours to Denver, and met Paula and David the next day.

Paula called Dave and Bette Haerther, at that time the owners of the land where the crash occurred, and asked if they had seen Bill's silver and gold fossil watch which had never been recovered. "Oh my," Betty gasped. "We did find a watch that matches your description perfectly."

After walking around the accident scene, Dave Haerther took Paula and David to a part of the crash site that contained a lot of debris. He walked over to a piece of plywood, kicked it up with his foot, and there was Bill's watch. He explained that he had discovered it a few days before and felt he should not move it. He then put it under the board, hoping that no one would take it before the rightful owners came along.[3]

The partially crushed watch sits hidden in a back corner of a dresser drawer that used to hold Bill's socks. Now it holds my sweaters and this one last precious reminder. The watch shows January 27, and is forever stuck at 5:28 p.m., what I assume to have been Bill's final moment on this earth.

In April of 2001, the Oklahoma legislature honored the plane crash victims during a special session at the State Capitol. Even though we shared a similar situation, I found it especially tough seeing the other families there, some with babies, others widowed like me, parents now without their children, other sons, like Amanda, suddenly without their fathers. I sensed the same hurt in Amanda, and yet, at the same time, I shared with her the pride we both felt for Bill. While Coach Sutton and President Halligan spoke, I stood on the floor of the State Senate, taking it all in, as tears streamed down my face.

When we left the building, a stranger walked up and said, "Mrs. Teegins, could I give you this $20 bill? I want to treat you and your daughter to lunch." When I protested, he said, "It would please me greatly, then, if you would use it for her college education." Something inside me shifted, nudged me to say yes. He was thrilled when I accepted the money, some part of him wanting to step into our space of shared sorrow. Similarly, such cards and letters came to the house. An elderly couple sent two dollars, explaining they were on a limited income and wished that they could give more. When I read their note, I sat at my kitchen table—too clean now, always too cleared off without Bill's sports journals and newspapers—rested my head on my arms and cried. One man had welded a cross and given it to Amanda to place in the ground at the crash site, which she had done when she accompanied Paula and David to Colorado.

On August 24th, 2001, feeling a bit more ready, I did travel with Amanda to Colorado to join family and friends for the dedication of a memorial located near the crash site. Gary Sparks, a 1966 OSU graduate in architecture, designed the beautiful 40 by 50-foot granite and marble memorial. The site, which is located approximately 25 miles east of Denver and a bit north of Interstate 70, near the town of Strasburg, Colorado, is bordered on three sides by a black wrought iron fence, with the fourth side open to visitors. The names and information about the 10 men killed at that spot are inscribed in slabs of granite.

Comanche Livestock Company owned the land upon which the memorial was built. Dave and Betty Haerther have since donated the land to OSU for its perpetual care.

August 25th, 2001, which would have been our 28th wedding anniversary, was a dark, gray day, not Colorado's usual gorgeous summer offering. I had feared this would be the case and, because of the personal significance of the date to me, I had tried to get the dedication changed, but OSU's fall term was beginning, and university officials had no other choice. Robert Boczkiewicz described the scene perfectly for *The Daily*

Part of the Strasburg, Colorado, memorial features a wonderful tribute to Bill. Inscribed on the granite marker is Bill's designation as "Voice of the Cowboys," along with the statement, "His family, friends, and fans will always remember, 'He shoots, he scores, heee's fouled!'" Gan Mathews, and his wife, Nancy, placed a rose on the engraved likeness of Bill and snapped this photograph after they noticed that someone had left a "Beat OU" license plate above Bill's marker.

Oklahoman, "Light rain and rumbling thunder mirrored the agonizing grief that pervaded the field of death."[4]

For the first few months after Bill's death, even if I made it through the middle of the day, put clothes on and ran errands, or attended one of the many recognition ceremonies, I went to bed crying—and I woke up crying. My first emotion each morning was emptiness—like I had this huge hole in my heart, or maybe no heart left at all, just a huge hole. I'd see husbands and wives holding hands in the stores or at the mall and I would have to leave, or at least sit down for a few minutes. It upset me to go into a Hallmark store and see all the cards to husbands for Valentine's Day, birthdays, and wedding anniversaries.

The first time I dropped clothes off at the cleaners that Bill and I used, the ladies gathered around me and we hugged and had tears together. I thought of the day that Bill and I fought over which one of us had to get out of the car and take the clothes into the cleaners, since we both had just gotten up and barely even brushed our teeth. Bill had on his ragged, blue warm-up suit and a frayed baseball cap to hide his hair that was still going in all directions. I wore old, faded walking shorts and a t-shirt and had no make-up on.

"You definitely look better than I do," Bill had joked. Therefore, I grabbed the bag but decided that this chore was going to backfire on him! I told the sweet ladies inside about our situation, and one of them made it a point to come out of the cleaners, tap on Bill's car window just so she could see how bad he looked off camera and in his casual, leisurely morning at-home attire. She even insisted that he let her take a peek under the hat.

For many months after Bill's death, I seldom left the house without someone—stranger or friend—coming up to give me a hug, or asking how I was doing? How was Amanda doing? Facing people for the first time after the accident was difficult and uncomfortable for us, and I'm sure it was for them, too.

In our attempts to begin leading our new "normal" lives, Amanda and I leaned on faith, family, friends, and each other. We made decisions that had not ever entered our minds a few months before. Amanda dropped out of her real estate studies at St. Cloud State University in Minnesota and came home. She enrolled in management courses at OSU, but she did keep her real estate interest alive the next summer by working at Oak Tree Country Club Realty in Edmond with broker Mariana Verga Lloyd, who literally took Amanda under her motherly wing.

At the suggestion of friends, I sought counseling with Ann Benjamin in Edmond and Amanda was counseled by one of Ann's associates. The counseling probably saved my life and it certainly helped me through the toughest times. Still, it was a full year before I could wean myself from the anti-depressants prescribed by doctors.

Ann remembers how broken I was—the many thoughts I was having, "How do I function without my soul-mate, my co-captain, my life partner, my lover, and my best friend? What would Bill want me to do? Who can I trust? What is the map for this part of my journey?"[5]

I was too "antsy" to sit still, too nervous and at "loose ends" to complete even the simplest house projects. For months, I couldn't even take walks in our neighborhood, especially not the route that Bill and I had always taken. Too many memories, too many replayed conversations, too many neighbors either smiling at me, trying hard to let me be just another sweaty jogger on the block, or not smiling at me, sometimes turning away, not knowing what on earth to say to me.

Once, the lady who delivered Fed Ex packages to our door, stopped me, "I miss seeing you and Bill on your daily walks, strolling hand in hand," she said. "It was so sweet," It was sweet, I agreed. I did need exercise though, so I tried taking different streets, or driving to Hafer Park and walking there.

Even taking a normal bath in our bathroom could start the tears. I could be lying there reading some food magazine when I would realize that Bill was not around to change the washer in the leaking showerhead. Suddenly the magazine would be wet and wrinkly and I'd be a sobbing mess again. I would lay in the sudsy water and remember all the conversations Bill and I had—me sitting on the tub, or soaking, while he shaved. More than once, I would step out of the bath and realize I had forgotten to wash.

The first thing I had done after Amanda and I returned from Amarillo was to slide Bill's toothbrush, shaving cream, and razor into the trash. It was a strange, vaguely angry gesture, but something I had to do.

I recognized that if I could not be stronger, I could not help Amanda. My counselor Ann recalls, "Janis kept asking questions like 'What about Amanda? I am not okay so how can I help her when I feel like I am in quick sand? How much longer will I feel like this?'"

There were times when I felt it was the worst storm I could ever endure. I wondered if the damage was too extensive to ever recover.[6] But in April of the first year without Bill, I woke up one morning and felt as if I had turned the corner, had come to terms with my grief. I realized that I would never be the same, never be the Janis Tietgens whom I had been for so many years, and life without Bill would forever more be extremely different.

Getting out of the house that now felt too strangely quiet seemed the right move, but to do what? Go where? I thought about going back to work for Delta as a flight attendant—but, instead, chose to take extended leave in order to think about what I should really do, what I even wanted to do in this new life I was heading into.

At first, I did return to the airport as a customer service agent. But I only lasted a month because being around airplanes and at the airport was too much of a reminder of what we had just experienced. I decided to take some real time off, to do volunteer work for the Arthritis Foundation, and to pursue an old interest of mine—writing—beginning with writing a book about my life with Bill.

About this time, I also started reaching out to people I'd always loved, but for whom I frankly had never made much time. I grew close to my brother, Jim, and his wife, Charlene. She became the sister I had never had, and I grew to know and fully appreciate my brother's love for Amanda and for me. I visited them often in Colleyville, Texas, where they helped me escape for a while and take my mind off things at home. Jim and Charlene made many trips to Edmond and helped me re-landscape the yard Bill had previously cared for. We put in an herb and butterfly garden and a drip system for the pots that lined the patio and pool. We recruited some of Amanda's friends to plant flowers and move dirt. Suddenly we couldn't stop planting. We worked side by side for several, full, long days. After hot showers to sooth our aching backs and calloused hands, we'd go to Pearl's Lakeside or Red Rock Canyon Grill and have a great meal and un-wind, maybe discuss our next project or re-hash our week. The gardening and the interactions with Amanda, her friends, and with Jim, and Charlene were entirely therapeutic and they cheered me up to no end.

I will never forget Jim and Charlene's gesture of moving to Oklahoma City for seven months just so they could be with me, to help me with everything big and small. We painted the master bedroom a different color, a soothing mint green, anything to make it seem like I claimed it for me now, anything to make it different. Jim, Charlene, and Amanda pitched in with our good friends Jim and Patty Holmes with the huge task of having an estate sale.

In the end, the changes were not enough. I found that I could not stay in the house that Bill and I had chosen and loved so together. My dear brother and Charlene helped me sell the house and move into an apartment, which fit me better.

As Sue Monk Kidd says in her wonderful book, The Secret Life of Bees, "It is the peculiar nature of the world to go on spinning no matter what sort of heartbreak is happening." And life was spinning on.

OSU hired Dave Hunziker, the radio voice of Western Kentucky University, to replace Bill as the voice of the Cowboys. During the pre-game show of the first OSU football game against Southern Mississippi

University, the first time Dave had taken the microphone in his new role, I called him during a commercial break and told him Bill would be proud of him for working his way up the competitive broadcasting ladder. Dave later told a reporter that he was glad that the remainder of the pre-game show had been taped ahead of time because he was too deeply moved by our conversation to go on the air live. He also said he would never forget my call because he had been hesitant about even applying for the job because of the circumstances.[7]

The first Christmas after Bill died, Jim, Charlene, Amanda, and I packed our bags and headed for New Orleans, Louisiana—anything to get away from the expected media stories and the hurt and memories we now associated with this previously loved holiday.

On January 27, 2002, the first anniversary of Bill's death, I traveled with Jim and Charlene to the Shangri-La resort on Grand Lake in north-east Oklahoma. Then, in February of that second year, they treated me to a trip of a lifetime to Paris, France. We spent nine wonderful days touring art museums, shopping, and eating at first class restaurants.

On the first anniversary of the crash, OSU placed a wreath at the crash site of the memorial in Colorado.

Sadly, for me, by July of that second year, Jim and Charlene had moved to Tampa, Florida, but not before they had seen that I was definitely on my feet and feeling better about things. Then I started looking forward to visiting them in their new, beautiful surroundings.

Amanda and I spent the second Christmas with Jim, Charlene, Jim's son, Bryce, and his friend Michael on the sunny beaches of Tampa. Once again, we got through another holiday, purposely doing something creatively different, because, after all, things are different now.

In February of 2002, just minutes before the Oklahoma State-Colorado University game, a memorial to the 10 men lost in the tragedy was dedicated on the OSU campus. Bill's family, along with Jim, Charlene, Amanda, and I attended the ceremony that unveiled "We Will Remember," a statue of a kneeling cowboy with his hat in his hands. The statue is surrounded by three walls with the images of the 10 men and the same words from their families etched into black Indian granite of which the Colorado crash site memorial is made.

My brother, Jim, and his wife, Charlene, in 2001. They accompanied Amanda, the Tietgens' family, and Janis to Bill's induction into the Oklahoma Sports Hall of Fame. Jim currently works for Sci-tex as vice-president of sales and marketing. Charlene is president of the Gibson Group, Inc., her successful Tampa, Florida, home-based executive recruiting business.

In February of 2001, Amanda and Janis attended a fundraiser to honor Bill sponsored by KWTV and KJ-103 Radio in Oklahoma City.

There have been so many more honors for Bill. Nearly one million dollars has been contributed to OSU scholarship funds in Bill's name and the names of the other crash victims. I was invited to accept the Contribution to Amateur Football Award, presented by the Oklahoma chapter of the National Football Foundation and College Hall of Fame, Inc. Bill's name was added to the Freedom Forum's Journalists Memorial in Arlington, Virginia. The memorial contains the names of 1,475 journalists who died since 1812 covering the news.

So many people have worked tirelessly to make certain Bill is never forgotten. The Oklahoma City Community Foundation administers the Bill Teegins Memorial Fund. Its earnings benefit the Arthritis Foundation and a communications scholarship to OSU. David Griffin kindly established the fund as a way to help Oklahomans express their grief over the tragedy.

After Bill's death, due to the huge extent of the very kind attention and the truly well meaning notoriety—which I didn't always know how to receive—I seriously considered changing my name back to Gibson, my maiden name. Checkout clerks and people on the streets and in the stores made connections between my last name and the OSU tragedy, and often they broke into tears. I would be trying to be strong, trying to get through a whole day without crying, trying to move forward, but I was having to pat people on the back and tell them, "It's okay. We'll be okay." Suddenly I wanted anonymity. I wanted privacy.

In the end, I decided that I had been Janis Teegins, married to the man of my dreams, Bill Teegins, for 27 years and there was no reason good enough for me to change my name. It is, in the end, who I was and very much who I still am.

Bill's portrait that hangs in the Oklahoma Sports Hall of Fame, sponsored by the Jim Thorpe Association in Oklahoma City.

Bill was posthumously inducted into the Oklahoma Sports Hall of Fame in August of 2001. OSU basketball coach Eddie Sutton was Bill's presenter for the induction. Here, Coach Sutton joined Amanda and Janis. Bill would have been so proud because he had been on the committee that had selected the first inductees into the Sports Hall of Fame years earlier. Courtesy Jim Thorpe Association.

McBride Clinic and Bone & Joint Hospital present the

BILL TEEGINS MEMORIAL GOLF CLASSIC

Monday, September 17, 2001
Oklahoma City Golf & Country Club

PLATINUM SPONSOR

MidFirst Bank

GOLD SPONSORS

BancFirst · BOLDT BUILDS · Cathey Consultants, Inc.
Flowers Engineering Company · Oscar J. Boldt Construction Company USA · Commercial Federal Bank
The Daily Oklahoman / The Sunday Oklahoman · Digital Graphics · Everest Brothers
Merrill Lynch · GEMINI · Janis & Amanda Teegins · KM
OSU · Nephrology Consultants · OG&E
· Pharmacia · Smith, Carney & Co., p.c.

HOLE SPONSORS

Bank One • Bank of Nichols Hills • CPD Tech Pack
Cole & Reed • International Golf Discount • KOSU
Marconi Medical Systems, Inc. • Mercy Health Center
Mustang Fuel • OMRF • Peat Marwick
R.K. Black, Inc. • RMP Investments • Signs to Go
Stillwater National Bank

BILL TEEGINS MEMORIAL GOLF CLASSIC

ASSOCIATE SPONSORS

Ball Photography · FELLERS · KWTV 9

ARTHRITIS FOUNDATION®

RIGHT: Amanda and Janis with other members of Bill's family, working as volunteers at the first *Bill Teegins Memorial Golf Classic* in September of 2001. Left to right, standing, Carol and Bill Tietgens, Paula Tietgens Cole, Randy Cassimus, Eric Schroeder, Greg Blackwood, and Amanda. Janis is in front with Ed Murray.

Kirk Jewell, who went to high school with Bill, was chairman of the September 9, 2002 tournament. Janis served as co-chair. McBride Clinic and Bone and Joint Hospital, major sponsors of the tournament, and too many wonderful volunteers to mention, did an outstanding job to raise $75,000 for arthritis research, the number one crippling disease. More than 200 golfers played in the 2002 Classic at the beautiful Oklahoma City Golf and Country Club. Rain played havoc with the early morning flights of golfers, but a warm autumn sun broke through for the afternoon players, a picture perfect ending to a great tournament.

LEFT: In September of 2001, the Arthritis Foundation renamed their annual tournament *The Bill Teegins Memorial Golf Classic*. This promotion poster of Bill's golf shoes is one of Janis' favorites. He wore these shoes to several of his previous Arthritis Foundation golf tournaments. *Courtesy Oklahoma Chapter, Arthritis Foundation and McBride Clinic and Bone and Joint Hospital.*

RIGHT: Paula Cole, Bill's sister, left, with Janis and Diane King, eating dinner in July of 2001, the night Amanda threw out the first pitch at the Red Hawks game at the Bricktown Ballpark in Oklahoma City.

BELOW: Amanda and Janis kept busy attending banquets of organizations that wanted to honor Bill and his work as an award-winning sportscaster. Here they accept a plaque that Clayton Vaughn, with whom Bill worked in the 1980s at KOTV in Tulsa, presented commemorating Bill's induction into the Oklahoma Association of Broadcasters Hall of Fame.

ABOVE: Bill's parents, Bill and Carol Tietgens, have remained supportive of Amanda and Janis, who thank them eternally.

BELOW: After Bill's death, Janis became close friends with KWTV's Alex Cameron and his family, left to right, Sarah, Ann, Alex, and Scott. In 2002, Alex and Ann ran the Honolulu Marathon to benefit the Arthritis Foundation portion of Joints in Motion in Bill's honor. Janis went along for support and they had a great time.

RIGHT: In 2002, the Oklahoma Sports Museum in Guthrie established the Bill Teegins Excellence in Sports Broadcasting Award to recognize talented announcers with Oklahoma ties. The first winner was Chicago White Sox announcer John Rooney, right. John worked at radio stations in Okmulgee and Tulsa, Oklahoma, and was the voice of the Oklahoma City 89ers and Oklahoma City University basketball in the early 1980s.

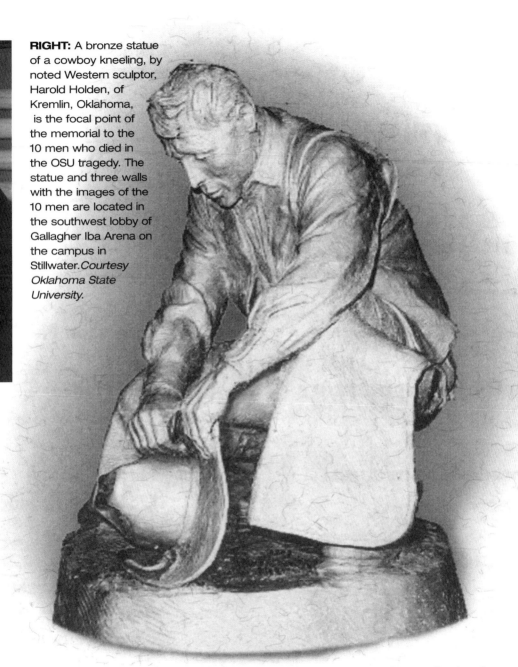

RIGHT: A bronze statue of a cowboy kneeling, by noted Western sculptor, Harold Holden, of Kremlin, Oklahoma, is the focal point of the memorial to the 10 men who died in the OSU tragedy. The statue and three walls with the images of the 10 men are located in the southwest lobby of Gallagher Iba Arena on the campus in Stillwater. *Courtesy Oklahoma State University.*

LEFT: Randy Johnson, the great left-handed pitcher for the Arizona Diamondbacks, visits with Richard Hendricks, left, and with Janis at a reception for Randy at the Oklahoma Sports Museum in Guthrie in January of 2003. Randy was in town to receive the Warren Spahn Award at the annual banquet held at the Masonic Lodge in Guthrie. Amanda and Janis presented Bobby Murcer, the great New York Yankee centerfielder and now broadcaster, the second annual Bill Teegins Excellence in Sports Broadcasting Award.

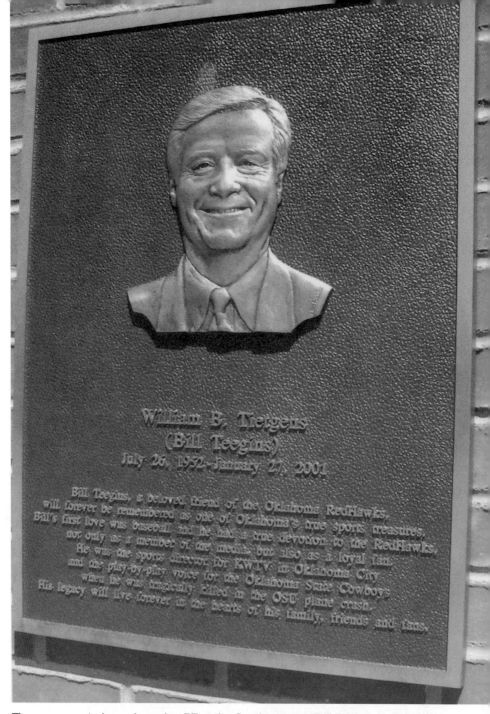

The permanent plaque honoring Bill at the Southwestern Bell Bricktown Ballpark in Oklahoma City. The plaque was the idea of Oklahoma City RedHawks' general manager Tim O'Toole to commemorate the special friendship Bill shared with the ball club. The plaque is adjacent to the Mickey Mantle statue. *Courtesy Eric Dabney*

LEFT: Amanda graduated from Oklahoma State University on May 10, 2003, with a bachelor's degree in business administration with a major in management. She immediately landed a job as a credit manager at Wells Fargo Financial in Tulsa.

BELOW: On January 21, 2003, Amanda surprised Janis on her 50th birthday with a party at Lottinville's in Edmond. Thirty of Janis' best friends also attended the celebration.

The memorial services and the great show of love and respect that came Bill's way in the weeks and months following his death would have embarrassed Bill, forever a modest man, not overly impressed with "ceremony." He had always told Ed Murray and Greg Blackwood, "If I die, don't make a big deal about it…just go on!"8 Lots of people made a big deal about it and, looking back, I'm glad they did. Bill deserved it. Now it's time to do as he said—it's time to go on.

I would like to thank you for letting me share a glimpse of my life with Bill Teegins. I hope that you carry with you not only Bill's memory, but also his love for God and family, his tremendous zest for life, and his innate generosity toward others. On days when I catch myself still brooding about life's nasty surprises, looking at the glass as half empty instead of so wonderfully full—as Bill always saw life—I have to stop and remember what I know above all about Bill Teegins—HE GOT IT!

CHAPTER 1:
A Minnesota Beginning
1. Interview with William Edward Tietgens and Carol Tietgens, January 4, 2003, hereinafter referred to as Bill and Carol Tietgens interview, Heritage Archives, Oklahoma Heritage Association, Oklahoma City, Oklahoma, hereinafter referred to as Heritage Archives.

2. Vold's Family Tree- 1827 to 1992, unpublished, Heritage Archives.

3. Bill Teegins baby book, Heritage Archives.

4 Ibid.

5. Bill and Carol Tietgens interview.

6. Ibid.

7. *St. Paul Sunday Pioneer Press* (St. Paul, Minnesota), December 6, 1959.

8. Bill and Carol Tietgens interview.

9. Ibid.

10. *The Daily Oklahoman*, July 16, 2000.

11. Ibid.

12. Bill and Carol Tietgens interview.

13. Bill Teegins scrapbook.

14. Ibid.

CHAPTER 2:
Moving to Oklahoma
1. Bill and Carol Tietgens interview.

2. Ibid.

3. Ibid.

4. Bill Tietgens scrapbook.

5. Interview with Elven Lindblad, January 15, 2003, hereafter referred to as Elven Lindblad interview, Heritage Archives.

6. Ibid.

7. Interview with Wayne McCombs, January 20, 2003, hereafter referred to as Wayne McCombs interview, Heritage Archives.

8. Ibid.

9. Ibid.

10. Elven Lindblad interview.

11. Wayne McCombs interview.

CHAPTER 4: Off to West Texas
1. Bill Tietgens interview, Heritage Archives.

2. Ibid.

3. Ibid.

CHAPTER 5: Back Home
1. Undated news clipping in the Bill Teegins scrapbook, Heritage Archives.

2. Elven Lindblad interview, Heritage Archives.

3. Wayne McCombs interview, Heritage Archives.

4. Ibid.

5. Elven Lindblad interview, Heritage Archives.

6. Wayne McCombs interview, Heritage Archives.

7. Interview with Eddie Day, March 10, 2003, hereinafter referred to as the Eddie Day interview, Heritage Archives.

8. Ibid.

9. Interview with Amanda Tietgens, April 9, 2003, hereinafter referred to as Amanda Tietgens interview, Heritage Archives.

CHAPTER 6: Oklahoma City
1. *The Daily Oklahoman*, March 10, 1987.

2. Interview with Ed Murray, January 15, 2003, hereinafter referred to as Ed Murray interview, Heritage Archives.

3. Ibid.

4. Memo from Paula Walker to staff, March 6, 1987, Heritage Archives.

5. *Tulsa World* (Tulsa, Oklahoma), March 6, 1987.

6. Kenny Franks, Paul Lambert, and Bob Burke, Historic Oklahoma: An Illustrated History (San Antonio, Texas: Historical Publishing Network, 2000), p. 245.

7. Ibid.

8. Amanda Tietgens interview.

9. Interview with Randy Cassimus, March 1, 2003, hereinafter referred to as Randy Cassimus interview, Heritage Archives.

10. Ibid.

11. Ed Murray interview, Heritage Archives.

12. Interview with Gary England, April 1, 2003, hereinafter referred to as Gary England interview, Heritage Archives.

13. Ed Murray interview.

14. Ibid.

15. Gary England interview.

16. Ibid.

17. Ed Murray interview.

18. Ibid.

19. Ibid.

20. *Tulsa World*, February 1, 1991.

21. *The Daily Oklahoman*, March 3, 1991.

22. Interview with Jason Price, January 1, 2003, hereinafter referred to Jason Price interview, Heritage Archives.

23. Ibid.

24. Letter from Bill Teegins to Oklahoma Department of Rehabilitative Services, July 19, 2000, Heritage Archives.

25. *The Daily Oklahoman,* January 29, 2001.

26. Ibid.

27. Ibid.

CHAPTER 7:
Voice of the Cowboys
1. *The Daily Oklahoman,* February 8, 1991.

2. Ed Murray interview.

3. *The Daily Oklahoman,* May 14, 1991.

4. Ibid.

5. Ibid., July 23, 1991.

6. Ibid.

7. Ibid.

8. Ibid. July 16, 2000.

9. Ibid.

CHAPTER 8:
Dreaming of a Tiki Hut
1. Interview with Greg Blackwood, January 17, 2003, herinafter referred to as Greg Blackwood interview.

2. Ibid.

3. Interview with Kelly Ogle, January 26, 2003, hereinafter referred to as Kelly Ogle interview, Heritage Archives.

4. Ibid.

5. Ibid.

6. Ibid.

7. Ibid.

8. Greg Blackwood interview.

9. Letter from Lisa Liebl to Janis Tietgens, March 25, 2003, Heritage Archives.

10. Ibid.

11. Ibid.

12. Interview with Suzi Clowers, March 10, 2003, hereinafter referred to as Suzi Clowers interview, Heritage Archives.

13. Ibid.

14. Ibid.

15. Ibid.

16. Interview with Stan Chase, March 1, 2003, hereinafter referred to as Stan Chase interview, Heritage Archives.

17. Ibid.

CHAPTER 9: Winds of Change
1. David Griffin interview, Heritage Archives.

2. Ibid.

3. Ibid.

4. *The Daily Oklahoman,* August 7, 1997.

5. Ibid.

6. Kelly Ogle interview, Heritage Archives.

7. Ibid.

8. News release, KWTV, September 15, 1997, Heritage Archives.

9. Letter from Lisa Liebl to Janis Tietgens, March 25, 2003, Heritage Archives.

10. David Griffin interview, Heritage Archives.

11. Ibid.

12. Ibid.

13. *The Daily Oklahoman,* July 16, 2000.

14. Ibid.

15. David Griffin interview, Heritage Archives.

16. *The Daily Oklahoman,* July 16, 2000.

17. Ibid., January 22, 1998.

18. E-mail from Paige Keithly to Eric Dabney, March 28, 2003, Heritage Archives.

CHAPTER 10:
Tragedy in Colorado
1. *The Daily Oklahoman,* January 2, 2001.

2. Greg Blackwood interview, Heritage Archives.

3. Amanda Tietgens interview.

4. *The Daily Oklahoman,* January 28, 2001.

5. Ibid.

6. *The Daily Oklahoman,* January 23, 2003.

7. *The Daily Oklahoman,* January 29, 2001.

8. Ibid.

9. Greg Blackwood interview, Heritage Archives.

10. Ibid.

11. Ibid.

12. Amanda Tietgens interview, Heritage Archives.

13. Kelly Ogle interview, Heritage Archives.

14. Ibid.

CHAPTER 11: The Aftershock
1. Interview with Alex Cameron, March 1, 2003, hereinafter referred to as Alex Cameron interview, Heritage Archives.

2. Ibid.

3. Transcript of KWTV 10:00 p.m. newscast, January 27, 2001, Heritage Archives.

4. Interview with Bill Merickel, January 18, 2003, Heritage Archives.

5. Alex Cameron interview.

6. Letter from Terry Alexander to Janis Tietgens, February 12, 2003, Heritage Archives.

7. Ibid.

8. Ibid.

CHAPTER 12:
Heartfelt Response
1. Cards, letters, and e-mails sent to Janis and Amanda Tietgens or KWTV, Heritage Archives.

2. Letter from Frank Keating to Janis Tietgens, February 7, 2001, Heritage Archives.

3. Letter from Kirk Humphreys to Janis Tietgens, February 15, 2001, Heritage Archives.

4. Letter from J.C. Watts, Jr., to Janis Tietgens, January 29, 2001, Heritage Archives.

5. Letter from Jean Carnahan to Janis Tietgens, February 6, 2001, Heritage Archives.

6. *The Daily Oklahoman,* January 30, 2001.

7. Bob Losure interview, Heritage Archives.

8. E-mail From Kate Sandefur to KWTV, January 29, 2001, Heritage Archives.

9. *The Daily Oklahoman,* January 29, 2001.

10. Ibid.

11. Cards, letters, and e-mails sent to Janis and Amanda Tietgens or KWTV, Heritage Archives.

12. Ibid.

13. Ibid.

14. Ibid.

15 Ibid.

16. Ibid.

17. *Legacy* (Stillwater, Oklahoma), published by the Oklahoma State University Foundation, Spring, 2001.

18. *Tulsa Cityscape* (Tulsa, Oklahoma), Vol. 3, No. 3, March, 2001, p. 48.

19 Ibid.

20 Ibid.

21 Ibid.

22 Ibid.

CHAPTER 13:
The Empty Chair
1. Transcript of KWTV newscast, January 28, 2001, Heritage Archives.

2. Ibid.

3. Ibid.

4. Ibid.

5. Ibid.

6. Ibid.

7. Ibid.

8. Ibid.

9. Transcript of David Griffin meeting with KWTV employees, January 30, 2001, Heritage Archives.

10. Ibid.

11. *The Daily Oklahoman,* February 2, 2001.

12. Ibid.

13. Ibid.

14. Transcript of the funeral service of William B. Tietgens, February 2, 2001, Heritage Archives.

15. Ibid.

16. Ibid.

17. Ibid.

18. Ibid.

19. Ibid.

20. Ibid.

21. Ibid.

CHAPTER 14: Going On
1. www.okstate.ocsn.com

2. www.baylorbears.ocsn.com

3. Paula Cole interview, Heritage Archives.

4. *The Daily Oklahoman,* August 26, 2001.

5. Interview with Ann Benjamin, January 15, 2003, Heritage Archives.

6. Ibid.

7. *The Daily Oklahoman,* January 26, 2002.

8 Greg Blackwood interview.

NEWSPAPERS AND PERIODICALS

Amarillo News, Amarillo, Texas

New York Times, New York, New York

Norman Transcript, Norman, Oklahoma

Denver Post, Denver, Colorado

Sports Collector Digest, New York, New York

Sports Illustrated, New York, New York

St. Paul Pioneer-Dispatch, St. Paul, Minnesota

Stillwater News Press, Stillwater, Oklahoma

The Daily Oklahoman, Oklahoma City, Oklahoma

The Daily O'Collegian, Stillwater, Oklahoma

The Sporting News, St. Louis, Missouri

The Sunday Oklahoman, Oklahoma City, Oklahoma

Tulsa Tribune, Tulsa, Oklahoma

Tulsa World, Tulsa, Oklahoma

BOOKS

Baird, David and Danney Gobel. *The Story of Oklahoma.* Norman: University of Oklahoma Press, 1994.

Bucek, Jeanine. *The Baseball Encyclopedia. 10th edition.* New York: MacMillan, 1996.

Burke, Bob. *Oklahoma: The Center of It All.* Encino, California: Cherbo Publishing Company, 2002.

Burke, Bob and Kenny A. Franks. *Abe Lemons: Court Magician.* Oklahoma City: Oklahoma Heritage Association, 1999.

Burke, Bob, Kenny A. Franks, and Royse Parr. *Glory Days of Summer: The History of Baseball in Oklahoma.* Oklahoma City: Oklahoma Heritage Association, 1999.

Franks, Clyda. *Tulsa.* Chicago: Arcadia Publishing, 2001.

Franks, Kenny A., Paul Lambert, and Bob Burke. *Historic Oklahoma.* San Antonio, Texas: Lammberts Publications, 1999.

Kahn, Roger. The Head Game: *Baseball Seen from the Pitchers Mound.* New York, Hartcourt, 2000.

Losure, Bob. *Five Seconds to Air.* Franklin, Tennessee: Hillsboro Press, 1998.

COLLECTIONS

Archives, KOTV, Tulsa, Oklahoma

Archives, KWTV, Oklahoma City, Oklahoma

Archives, Oklahoma Association of Broadcasters, Oklahoma City, Oklahoma

Archives, Oklahoma Heritage Association, Oklahoma City, Oklahoma.